Saratoga
IN *Bloom*

150 YEARS OF GLORIOUS GARDENS

Janet Loughrey

DownEastBooks

Camden, Maine

Published by Down East Books

An imprint of Rowman & Littlefield

4501 Forbes Boulevard, Suite 200, Lanham, Maryland 20706

www.rowman.com

10 Thornbury Road, Plymouth PL6 7PP, United Kingdom

Distributed by National Book Network

British Library Cataloguing in Publication Information Available

Library of Congress Cataloging-in-Publication Data

The hardback edition of this book was previously cataloged by the Library of Congress as follows:

Loughrey, Janet.

   Saratoga in bloom : 150 years of glorious gardens / Janet Loughrey.

     p. cm.

   1. Historic gardens—New York (State)—Saratoga. I. Title.

   SB466.U65S282 2010

                         2009052976

ISBN : 978-0-89272-798-8 (cloth : alk. paper)

ISBN : 978-1-60893-260-3 (pbk : alk.paper)

ISBN : 978-0-89272-988-3 (electronic)

Designed by Lynda Chilton

∞™ The paper used in this publication meets the minimum requirements of
American National Standard for Information Sciences—Permanence of Paper
for Printed Library Materials, ANSI/NISO Z39.48-1992.

Printed in China

*To
Victoria and Teri,
whose generosity
will never
be forgotten.*

Contents

Cut flowers for sale at the Saratoga Farmers' Market

Foreword

Janet Loughrey has captured the essence of what makes Saratoga Springs the summer destination that it is. Written with passion and accuracy, *Saratoga in Bloom* doesn't just tell you about the city and its gardens, it shows you. Many Spa City residents may be aware that fabulous floral displays once graced grand estates, but Janet brings us old images of the elaborate gardens that once commanded the attention of passersby. She has weeded through old newspaper and magazine clippings, followed little glimmers of stories, and talked with the people who remember stories about gardens and gardeners now gone. There are quirky tales, sad stories, and admirable accounts.

I found myself studying the photographs and wondering where this garden stood, what that plant was. I also found myself smiling over the fact that the Victorian fascination with cannas, elephant ears, and other tropicals has resurfaced, and these plants are once again popular in our parks and on our boulevards.

There's a lot to Saratoga Springs beyond horse racing and mineral springs. The area's geologic history includes the petrified sea gardens, the sandy soils that are the perfect habitat for the endangered Blue Karner butterfly, and, of course, the springs that brought the first crowds to partake of the waters during the Victorian age.

Saratoga Springs is fortunate to have these distinctive assets of the past still present today. There are grand old mansions, wide streets, the country's oldest race course, pavilions protecting bubbling springs, and places in Saratoga State Park where you can still collect mineral water in bottles. It is a city where the past and present are both valued.

It is also a city that takes pride in looking good. Beds of blooms line sidewalks, abundant baskets hang from the lampposts, and window boxes decorate storefronts. Just as the socialites don fancy hats and frocks for the track season and summer galas, the city dresses up for the summer crowds. Janet introduces us to some of the people behind all this beauty, from the century-old floral business that grows the seedlings that will decorate the Saratoga Race Course clubhouse and grounds, to the city's "flower power" downtown displays, to the welcoming entrance gardens at Saratoga Spa State Park, the roses at Yaddo, and the private gardens of some of the accomplished gardeners who live and garden here.

As a north country native, Janet appreciates how challenging it is to nurture a garden here. When you look at the photographs, and realize this is northern New York, zone 5, you can't help marveling at the gardens and the great efforts of the gardeners who created them despite beastly winters and hail-wielding summer thunderstorms.

Everyone has heard of Saratoga Springs for its place in the Revolutionary war, its healing waters, or its historic race track. Now thanks to *Saratoga in Bloom*, they'll get to know its gorgeous gardens.

Natalie Walsh

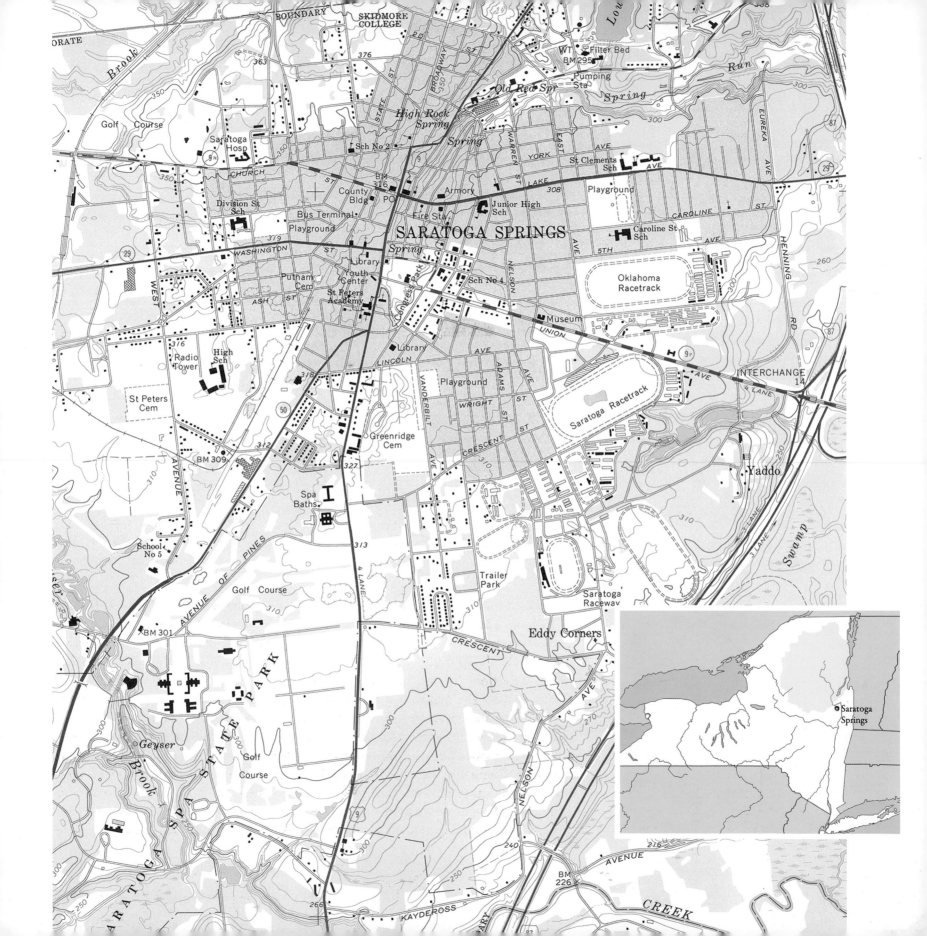

THE *Spa City: America's Resort*

Located thirty miles north of Albany in the bucolic upstate region of New York State, Saratoga Springs is filled at once with history, natural beauty, architectural splendor, and colorful lore. This small community, halfway between Montreal and New York City, has reinvented itself many times since its inception, and it remains a world-class destination and the home of some twenty-eight thousand year-round residents. Nestled between the foothills of the Adirondack Mountains and the romantic farmlands of the Hudson River Valley, Saratoga Springs was greatly influenced by its unique geology.

Deep below the earth's crust, under layers of shale and dolomitic limestone, lies an ancient sea. As the glaciers of the ice age receded ten thousand years ago, the shifting earth developed fractures in the rocky stratum. The seawaters percolated, pushed, and seeped to the surface through the layers and cracks, creating spouters and pools laced with rich minerals. The springs arose from fissures in the Saratoga Fault, which extends south for sixty-five miles from Whitehall to Albany. Salts were leached from the underground limestone

MAP COURTESY OF U.S. GEOLOGICAL SURVEY, C. 1967.
Opposite: Lawn jockeys, such as this example at the home of Denise Herman, are an integral part of the Saratoga landscape.

and the waters were infused with carbon dioxide, creating the same effervescent bubbles found in today's carbonated drinks.

The springs found in the Saratoga region represent the only active spouting geyser east of the Mississippi River, and the only naturally carbonated springs between the Rocky Mountains and Europe's legendary spas. The water temperature remains a constant 55 degrees Fahrenheit (13 degrees Celsius), differentiating these springs from the true hot-water geysers of the western United States.

Native Mohawk tribes, part of the Iroquois Confederacy, were the first known inhabitants of the region. They believed that the waters of the mineral springs held great spiritual, medicinal, and health-giving powers. They named the area Sarachtogue, meaning "the place near swift water," in reference to its proximity to the mighty Hudson River.

Europeans first settled here around the time of the Revolutionary War. Battles fought at Saratoga in 1777 were widely considered the turning point of the war. Sir William Johnson was purported to be the first to view the springs at Saratoga when he visited High Rock in 1771. Other discoveries followed, including that of Congress Spring, which would play a crucial role in shaping the town's future.

To accommodate the visitors who flocked to the region to drink and bathe in the restorative waters, lumberman Gideon Putnam established the first hotel, Putnam's Tavern and Boarding House. He was also instrumental in the town's planning, designing the main street and setting aside land for churches, schools, cemeteries, and parks.

When Dr. John Clarke started bottling Congress Spring waters and selling them throughout the United States and Europe, he put Saratoga on the national and international map. He cleared the land around the spring and built pathways where visitors could walk off the effects of their liquid therapy.

As Saratoga's reputation grew as a place of healing, it evolved into a premier resort destination. The settlement was established as a town in 1819 and incorporated as a village in 1826. Putnam's tavern was expanded into the larger Union Hall, which became the Union Hotel, and finally reopened as the Grand Union Hotel in 1874. It was the world's largest hotel at the time, with more than seven hundred rooms. Other resorts, each rivaling the size and grandeur of the previous, were constructed to serve the growing legion of tourists. Architectural marvels of their time, these magnificent hotels evolved from merely places to sleep into destinations in and of themselves.

Because transportation was primitive, and the journey from large cities such as Boston and New York was long and arduous, tourists stayed for several weeks or more. Among the more illustrious early visitors were George Washington, John Quincy Adams, Joseph Bonaparte (former king of Spain and brother of Napoleon), and Ulysses S. Grant.

An important aesthetic of these early resorts was the grand courtyard, landscaped with

Center: Columbian Spring, in Congress Park, is one of Saratoga's many famous mineral springs. *Opposite:* The park was the center of Saratoga Springs during its heyday as a health spa, and the grand hotels were located close by. COURTESY SARATOGA ROOM, SARATOGA LIBRARY

elaborate gardens. The expansive spaces were adorned with neatly manicured lawns and formal flower beds, in the European style of the day. Guests could walk, socialize, and relax on long park benches. Completing the richly embellished landscapes were oversize classic fountains and urns planted with brightly colored annuals.

Many of the grand hotels were located near Congress Spring Park, as it was then called, which became the centerpiece of this vibrant resort as its landscaping was continually upgraded with lavish ornamental plantings, water features, and classic statuary. Strolling along the park's meandering pathways, with leisurely breaks on the park benches, was a favorite activity. The park became a fashionable place to see and be seen.

Several miles east of town, lake houses were built on the shores of Lake Lonely and Saratoga Lake, where regattas were held and patrons could fish, swim, and boat. One of the most notable resorts was Moon's Lake House, where the iconic American food known as the potato chip was invented. Other small boarding houses, such as The Old Homestead, handled overflow from the more popular resorts. The homestead grounds were said to be landscaped with some fifty thousand flowers.

Fine dining, along with big-name entertainment and stage shows, was a big draw to the lake houses built later on, many of which were colorfully landscaped but thinly disguised gambling parlors. The backroom gambling activities attracted a gamut of patrons, from seasonal tourists to notorious gangsters who represented a seamier side of Saratoga's leisure activities. The lake houses are gone, but their memory lives on. Dude Dehn, fourth-generation owner of Dehn's Flowers, a local business operating since 1892, recalls his father and grandfather decorating the more prominent lake house properties, including

Piping Rock, Riley's, The Brook, and Newman's, with flowers.

Saratoga's reputation as a fashionable playground for the wealthy—rivaling Newport, Rhode Island, as the nation's "social capital"—was cemented by improved steamship and railroad service in the 1820s and 1830s. Illustrious families such as the Vanderbilts and Whitneys, and notable figures such as Diamond Jim Brady and Lillian Russell, made Saratoga a regular destination. Wall Street financier Spencer Trask and his wife, Katrina, built their estate, named Yaddo, on the outskirts of town. The couple would designate that the property be used as an artist colony, also bequeathing the community a significant public garden in the process.

As high-society aristocrats spent more time in Saratoga, they built summer "cottages," which were often elaborate and imposing mansions. The concentration of elegant homes along North Broadway, Circular Street, Union Avenue, and other centrally located city streets represents one of the largest collections of fine Victorian mansions in the United States. Many of these continue as part-time summer residences for the well heeled.

Amusements, an important part of the vacation experience during the 1800s, included dances, parties, and sporting events. Gambling, although controversial, was introduced in 1835. Famed prizefighter and congressman Jim Morrissey opened The Clubhouse, a men's gambling parlor, near Congress Spring Park in 1862. (It's thought that the club sandwich was invented here.) Following the introduction of harness racing in 1847, Morrissey and William R. Travers (a successful Wall Street broker) were part of a group who organized

the first thoroughbred horse race meet. The year was 1863. The event was extremely popular, and the men began developing the Saratoga Race Course the following year.

As Saratoga continued to evolve into one of America's premier resort destinations, another use for its legendary springs was discovered. During the 1890s, a method was developed to extract carbonic acid from the waters, which was a key ingredient in carbonated soft drinks and ice-cream sodas. The new beverages became wildly popular, and gas and bottling plants were constructed to meet the ensuing demand.

The city made famous for its mineral springs became known by a variety of nicknames, including "The Spa," "Spa City," and "Queen of Spas." Locals today often refer to the city as simply "Saratoga."

The 1890s represented a shift for Saratoga Springs. Searching for new ways to entice visitors and extend the tourist season, an annual floral fête was held, celebrating the Victorian era of flowers. Businesses were decked out with greenery and blooms, and the city held a grand parade, a floral ball, and various pageants. With this stroke of civic genius, ornamental landscaping assumed a prominent and permanent role in shaping the ambiance of Saratoga.

The twentieth century was a time of boom and bust. Although the village was incorporated as a city in 1915, widespread travel in automobiles was by then beginning to diminish the resort's status as a premier destination. The era following World War II marked a decline. Business at the great hotels suffered, and most of them, including the United States Hotel and the Grand Union Hotel, were torn down. The stately elm trees that had graced the main street for more than a hundred years and contributed to its elegant character succumbed to Dutch elm disease.

But the cycle would reverse. In the 1960s, the Adirondack Northway, the interstate highway that connects Albany and Montreal, was completed. It offered easier access to once-remote areas and revitalized upstate New York cities. In addition, Saratoga Springs became known as a world-class cultural center with the establishment of Yaddo as a renowned artist colony, the expansion of Skidmore College's liberal arts programs, and the completion of the Saratoga Performing Arts Center (SPAC). The summer home of the New York City Ballet and the Philadelphia Orchestra, SPAC also draws top contemporary musical performers and other major acts. The Lake George Opera relocated to the nearby Spa Little Theater in 1998. The National Museum of Dance, established in historic Spa

Center: The Spirit of Life monument in 2002, before construction of the Congress Park Centre. *Above:* Plantings grace the landmark Adelphi Hotel on Broadway, the last of Saratoga's Victorian hotels.

Park, and the National Museum of Racing and Hall of Fame, across from the thorough-bred race course, also enhance the region's culture. In recent years, Beekman Street has become a haven for artist studios and fine galleries.

Along with this local renaissance, a beautification effort was born. Beginning in 1979, the city's commissioner of public works, in conjunction with a local schoolteacher, established a Flower Power program of planting flower beds around local streets and parks. Today, the program has a designated budget and a staff to keep the flowers watered, fed, and groomed during the peak summer months.

The city's efforts were contagious. Private businesses joined in on their own, adorning their storefronts with hanging baskets, planters, and flower beds. Residents followed suit, cultivating small urban plots, street-side borders, and porch-side gardens. For the throngs who flock to Saratoga in summer to enjoy the city's horse culture, the Saratoga Race Course, the Racino (Saratoga Gaming and Raceway), and the Fasig-Tipton Pavilion decorate their respective grounds with an array of annual and perennial flowers. Horse trainers and owners in town for the six-week thoroughbred meet spare no expense in decorating their seasonal homes with lovely landscaping for the short time they are in residence.

Saratoga's love of flowers and beautiful plantings have become as identifiable to the city as the mineral springs and the sport of horse racing. A style of gardening has emerged that is unique to this city: the use of Victorian urns, lawn jockeys, and classic statuary as focal points, combined with lots of bold-colored annuals, especially the iconic canna lily, and the lovely backdrop of historic architecture to set it all off.

The backdrop of historic downtown buildings, Victorian mansions, and the legendary race course have appeared in such Hollywood movies as *Ghost Story, Seabiscuit,* and *Billy Bathgate.* Caffé Lena, the oldest continuously operating coffeehouse in America, has hosted such legendary singers as Arlo Guthrie and Bob Dylan, and it's said that Don McLean penned his hit "American Pie" a few blocks away, at the venerable Tin & Lint. Carly Simon mentions the Spa City in her classic pop song "You're So Vain."

Today, the city of Saratoga Springs remains as vibrant as it was in its nineteenth-century heyday. The track and other popular local attractions continue to draw thousands of visitors each year. Much of the downtown has retained its vintage character. The grand mansions that line Union Avenue and North Broadway have been lovingly restored and preserved. The charming side streets, which manage to escape most of the traffic and bustle of racing season, contain an extraordinary mix of residential architecture. Urban neighborhoods such as Franklin Square and the Beekman Street art district comprise an eclectic mix of homes and shops. With its classic grandstand, paddocks, and backstretch, the thoroughbred racetrack looks much as it did many decades ago, when the great horses such as Man o' War, Citation, and Seabiscuit inspired legions of racing fans. Preservation organizations, civic groups, and local government collaborate to preserve a way of life that spurs a sense of community pride. If one had to sum up Saratoga Springs in just three words, the city's motto says it all: "Health, History, Horses." ❧

Saratoga's motto says it all.

North Country Gardening

The North Country, including the Saratoga region, is known for its long, harsh winters and fluctuating temperatures, both of which pose a challenge to plants. Most of Saratoga County is located in USDA Zone 4b, which means that average minimum winter temperatures can reach –20 to –25 degrees Fahrenheit (–29 to –32 degrees Celsius). Saratoga Springs and the southern tip of the county toward Schenectady is in USDA Zone 5a, with slightly warmer minimum temperatures of –15 to –20 degrees Fahrenheit (–26 to –29 degrees Celsius).

Terrain, snow cover, elevation, and winds also need to be considered. The topography around Saratoga ranges from the foothills of the southern Adirondacks in the west to the bucolic patchwork of open farmlands across much of the county. Elevation ranges from twenty feet above sea level in Waterford to 2,600 feet in the Adirondack foothills (Saratoga Springs is at 300 feet). Storms coming off the mountains often bring pelting precipitation and prodigious winds, although the deep snow cover typical of most winters insulates plants from extreme cold and allows plants from a zone or two warmer to survive in some years.

Soils in Saratoga County vary widely. The soil in downtown Saratoga Springs tends to be sandy, transitioning to more loam in areas outside of town. Clay soils are found farther out, and rocky soil predominates in the mountain foothills.

On average, the last frost-free date is May 20 and the average first frost occurs on September 20. Saratoga gardeners traditionally mark the Memorial Day weekend as the official start of the gardening season.

Choosing the right plant can mean the difference between success and failure. There are lots of hardy roses to choose from, such as Canadian Explorer, Buck, Meidilands, the Carefree series, and rugosas. The newer Knock Out series of landscape roses is proving to do well locally. Shrubs that bloom on the previous year's growth, such as mophead hydrangeas, may perform poorly. Newer hydrangea varieties such as *H. macrohylla* 'Endless Summer' bloom on both old and new wood, making them a good option. Sturdy old-fashioned Peegee hydrangeas *(H. paniculata* 'Grandiflora') are an even better choice.

Wild columbine (Aquilegia)

Reliable perennials that are commonly used by local gardeners include daylilies *(Hemerocallis),* hostas, bee balm *(Monarda),* coneflower *(Echinacea),* ox eye daisy *(Leucanthemum),* Joe-Pye weed *(Eupatorium),* black-eyed Susan *(Rudbeckia),* perennial sunflower *(Helianthus),* columbine *(Aquilegia),* and tickseed *(Coreopsis).* New versions of tried-and-true species include mildew-resistant bee balm, coneflowers in an array of colors and forms, and Joe-Pye weed with shorter stature or colored leaves. These new cultivars, bred by national companies, combined with plants such as daylilies and hostas hybridized by local growers, help local gardeners make their personal space unique.

Congress Park: Where It All Began

Congress Park, which sits at the center of the Spa City, is literally the spot where the community of Saratoga Springs was born more than two hundred years ago. The colorful story of the rise and fall of the park closely mirrors that of the community. The park, one of the oldest public outdoor spaces in the United States, is the heart and soul of the city itself—a gleaming jewel in an exquisite setting.

The park had dubious beginnings as an uninhabitable swamp. In 1792, Nicholas Gilman discovered Congress Spring, which was named in honor of his service during the First Continental Congress, in Philadelphia in 1774. The spring waters, thought to have restorative properties, were made available for public consumption.

Dr. John Clarke, one of Saratoga's most prominent citizens, purchased Congress Spring and the surrounding land in 1823. He built a bottling plant and sold the waters throughout the United States and Europe, enhancing Saratoga's status as a world-class destination. He drained the swamp and made improvements, creating a park with pathways, wide expanses of formal lawn, and a classic-style pavilion over the spring. Other springs were discovered nearby and to the south in Geyser Park.

Left: The World War I monument is the backdrop for the Thorvaldsen Night and Day vases at Congress Park. The benches and brick walkway are recent renovations.
Above: The vases sat in a different location at the time this postcard was made, back when the Grand Union Hotel still overlooked the park. Courtesy Saratoga Room, Saratoga Library

The visitors who came to drink and bathe in the healing waters were served by several grand hotels. Dipper boys and girls stationed at each spring dispensed glass cups of the mineral waters to passing visitors. Paths offered imbibers a place to stroll. As Saratoga's reputation grew, the park became a fashionable place for the social elite to be seen.

In 1876, Frederick Law Olmsted and Jacob Weidenmann were hired to renovate the park in honor of the nation's centennial. One of America's greatest landscape architects, Olmsted is best known for his designs of New York City's Central Park, the landscape surrounding the U.S. Capitol building in Washington, D.C., the Biltmore Estate in Asheville, N.C., and dozens of public parks and academic campuses, including Stanford University in California. Olmsted returned to Saratoga several times, seeking relief for his own health issues.

The new plan enhanced the naturally bucolic setting around Congress Spring with man-made ponds, a reservoir, meandering paths, and a covered promenade. Shrubs, trees, and flowers were installed, creating dramatic and attractive vistas. A Victorian bandstand, erected on the shore of one of the lakes, was the site of many outdoor concerts featuring notable musicians such as John Philip Sousa and Enrico Caruso. Among the more unusual features of Congress Park were an enclosed deer park, an Indian encampment, and a Japanese tea garden.

In 1870, famed prizefighter and former congressman John Morrissey acquired land adjacent to Congress Spring Park and built The Clubhouse, a men's gambling house. The property was later acquired by Richard Canfield, who made extensive improvements to the Italian-style brick building. He lavishly furnished the interior, adding custom stained-glass windows and an elegant dining hall.

Near the northeast corner of the property, Canfield made plans for a formal Italianate garden. The landscape was created at the suggestion of Canfield's friend Charles W. Eliot, then president of Harvard University. Canfield's head gardener, Frank De Frank, installed the design in 1902–03. Chiseled marble pieces were commissioned by Canfield and imported from Carrara, Italy. Four statues were made in the image of Greek gods, including Hermes, the messenger of gods, and Pan, a forest god. The centerpiece was a

Clockwise from left: A fiberglass horse painted by Chris O'Leary was part of the 2002 Horses, Saratoga Style project administered by the Saratoga County Arts Council; this one stood at the entrance to Congress Park. The World War I monument. A recently restored Victorian-era reservoir with Deer Park Spring in the background.

sundial modeled after one in Lugano, Italy. A pair of Corinthian-style columns marked the transition to the lower garden, and a large marble reflecting pool just beyond the columns featured two statues, known as *Spit and Spat.* The figures were made in the likeness of Triton (half man and half fish), son of the sea god Poseidon. Placed at opposite ends of the pool, the statues were positioned to playfully spout water toward each other through conch shell trumpets.

In 1911, when the state reservation was created to protect the area's mineral springs, the privately held Congress Spring Park was turned over to what was then the Village of Saratoga Springs. Following a vigorous antigambling movement, the casino owned by Richard Canfield had closed in 1907 and he had sold the property, which included the casino and the Italian gardens, to the village; it became the northeast section of Congress Spring Park. In 1912 and 1913, Congress Hall, a hundred-year-old hotel that had fallen on hard times, and John Clarke's adjacent bottling plant were razed. Putnam Street between Spring and Congress streets was closed, and this parcel was incorporated as the northwest portion of the park. Landscape architect Charles Leavitt was hired to create a master plan to integrate the three properties, expanding the park's area to its current size of twenty-one acres.

The Victorian arcades that housed Congress and Columbian springs were torn down, and Congress Spring was reconstructed into an open fountain set in a sunken garden. With the advent of the automobile, the Civil War monument was moved in 1921 from the

center of Broadway at the park entrance to its present location inside the park to protect it from possible damage from traffic.

The *Spirit of Life* monument, one of the most significant features of Congress Park, was completed in 1914 and installed at the former site of Congress Hall. The statue was created by Daniel Chester French (best known for his sculpture of Abraham Lincoln at the Lincoln Memorial in Washington, D.C.) and Henry Bacon, who designed the Lincoln Memorial. Katrina Trask, who owned the Yaddo estate with her husband, Spencer, commissioned the monument to commemorate her late husband, who was killed in a train accident in 1909.

The bronze figurine in the monument represents Hygieia, the ancient Greek goddess of health and cleanliness. A bowl in one hand symbolizes the health-restoring properties of the mineral springs, and the pine boughs she holds in her other hand represent the concept of longevity and the towering pines at Yaddo. The reflecting pool, made from Indiana

Left: The fountain featuring dueling tritons Spit and Spat is a beloved feature of Congress Park. *Above:* The newly restored Italian Gardens, completed in 2008, are a significant addition to the park and a nod to the city's penchant for historic preservation.

limestone, signifies the type of rock from which the area's mineral springs originate. The monument was inscribed with a personal motto that was dear to Spencer, "To do good and serve my fellow man." The posture of Hygieia, with her arms uplifted in jubilance, represents the spirit of Spencer Trask himself.

The memory of Spencer's wife, Katrina, who along with her husband established the artist colony at Yaddo, is immortalized at the southwestern corner of the park with an imposing granite staircase that was designed by the firm of Ludlow and Peabody in 1922. The staircase and entry columns were made of pink Adirondack granite; pink was Katrina's favorite color. The stone was excavated from the vicinity of Lake George, where the Trasks spent summers at their retreat on Triuna Island. The staircase was built by local stonemason Robert R. Ritchie; he had discovered a fossilized sea garden outside Saratoga and embedded some of the preserved fossils into the stone staircase.

Other park improvements included iron and stone gates at the park's entrance, constructed in the 1920s and dedicated to Senator Edgar T. Brackett in recognition of his efforts to protect the mineral springs. And in 1931 the Victorian bandstand, where musicians once entertained legions of tourists, was razed and a World War I memorial was dedicated in its place.

A Flower Thief in Our Midst

Attractive plantings, including colorful annual bedding plants, have long been part of Congress Park. An August 26, 1918, article in *The Saratogian* newspaper describes an elusive geranium thief, whose identity remained a mystery for weeks. The nighttime flower thefts became so rampant that George W. Ainsworth, commissioner of public works, assigned several detectives overnight duty to patrol the park.

Over a period of several nights, the geraniums continued to disappear right under the noses of the detectives. The men would hear a rustle and snap of flower stems, but by the time they came upon the crime scene, the offender was nowhere to be found.

On the final night, the detectives, ever more determined to catch the repeat offender in the act, drew their guns and lay in wait. When they heard the familiar rustling in the geranium beds, they sprang up—just in time to glimpse a dark flash disappearing into the nighttime shadows. They recognized the park alligator, its mouth full of geraniums, scurrying back to its home in one of the park's ponds.

How this tropical reptile ended up residing in the park, and the fate of the creature, are unknown. Nor is it clear what punishment was meted out to the scaly perpetrator for its role in committing this notable heist of the park's floral treasures.

Opposite: An octagonal building shelters an antique wooden horse carousel. Restored and reopened in 2002, the carousel is a favorite park attraction. *Top:* Over the years the plantings outside the Canfield Casino have been changed to a simpler layout that requires less maintenance. *Center:* A spray of water frames the granite Katrina Trask staircase. Completed in 1922, it is a memorial to one of Saratoga's most illustrious citizens.

Restoring a City's Gem

The park entered a period of decline beginning in 1939. Because of overpumping and the resulting contamination, Congress Spring was abandoned and covered with rocks and fill dirt. Other aspects of the park soon deteriorated, and embellishments such as vases, statues, and benches disappeared.

By the 1960s, much of the park had fallen into disrepair. Plantings were overgrown, remaining statuary was vandalized, and vagrants moved in. A low point was reached in 1963, when public works commissioner Charles McTygue had the *Spirit of Life* reflecting pool filled with dirt with the idea of turning it into a rose garden. McTygue claimed that the pool, which had suffered structural damage, was too expensive to repair. He felt

it was a public nuisance and a hazard to young children, as the basin had become a favorite repository for empty bottles and other trash. But his decision, made without the authorization of the mayor and city council, was viewed by local citizens as the desecration of an irreplaceable work of art. With the ensuing public outcry, the dirt was removed from the pool and replaced with water.

The 1970s marked the beginning of a new era for Congress Park. In 1976, a master plan, commissioned through the Office of Community Development, provided a detailed outline for the rehabilitation and long-range development of the park. This new phase was begun exactly one hundred years after Frederick Law Olmsted's centennial renovation, and two hundred years after John Clarke's first attempts at landscaping.

The city began clearing the undergrowth and repairing structures and adding new ones. A replica of John Clarke's original Congress Spring pavilion, an open structure with Doric columns, was built, and the spring, which had been buried in 1939, was allowed to flow again. As part of a citywide beautification effort, dubbed "Flower Power," blooming plants were installed around the park.

In the 1980s, as part of the continuing restoration of the park, the Italian gardens were renovated. The reflecting pool and *Spit and Spat* statues were refurbished, and symmetrical paths and planting beds were constructed. An overgrown hedgerow was removed and replaced with dwarf Alberta spruce. The *Spirit of Life* statue was restored, the process overseen by the Saratoga Springs Preservation Foundation. The masonry-and-limestone basin was repaired and the pool's drainage was improved. Consulting the 1914 blueprints

Spring blossoms at Congress Park: Tulips at the Broadway entrance, lilacs near the vintage carousel, and a 'Tina' crabapple near Deer Park Spring.

drawn by Charles Leavitt, park officials re-created the original plantings around the statue. Six arborvitaes were planted on either side of the reflecting pool, and sumac and spruce were planted along the wall. Pussy willow *(Salix discolor)* and white-flowering dogwood trees *(Cornus florida)* were installed between the stone seating and the adjacent pond.

During the 1970s and 1980s, more than a million dollars, much of it state and federal grant money, was used to restore the Canfield Casino. A multitiered fountain adjacent to the casino, installed by its original owner, John Morrissey, was refurbished in the late 1980s. Two small antique urns at the edge of the north pond were also restored at the same time. The now-glittering casino, the centerpiece of the park, is home to the Saratoga Springs History Museum. The lavish parlor and ballroom are rented out for private parties, weddings, and other events. The landscaping along the front, which has changed over the years, includes low-maintenance plants such as hostas, hydrangeas, and fall-blooming sedums. Nonhardy hibiscus shrubs are stored in greenhouses over the winter and placed (still in their pots) into the landscape in late spring.

One of the park's biggest modern-day advocates was former public works commissioner Thomas McTygue (son of earlier commissioner Charles McTygue) For thirty-t years until his retirement in 2007, he helped facilitate many of the most recent ren adhering to the 1976 master plan's concepts and objectives. McTygue wa

The massive yet grace-
ful Katrina Trask staircase
overlooks one of Con[...]
Park's ponds.

in developing the Flower Power campaign and increasing Saratoga's budget to expand the citywide planting program, which included Congress Park. He was also responsible for implementing the recent restoration of the Italian Gardens near the Canfield Casino.

Trees are an integral part of the park, with some fifty identified species. Varieties include evergreen conifers of fragrant balsam fir, white spruce, and northern white cedar. Deciduous trees include flowering dogwood, weeping willow, towering black walnut, several kinds of oak and maple, and the ancient ginkgo. Rows of pruned northern catalpa surround the *Spit and Spat* fountain. The diverse trees found in the park are expertly documented in a brochure produced by the Saratoga Mentoring Program.

One of the more delightful additions in recent years is the vintage carousel near the Spring Street entrance. The twenty-eight wooden horses, hand-carved by Russian artisan Marcus Illions, were part of a featured ride at Kaydeross Park, a former amusement venue on Saratoga Lake. The 1910 antique ride was rescued from dismantlement when Saratoga Springs offered the winning bid at a public auction in 1987. Private funds were raised to restore the carousel and build a new pavilion to house it, a process that took fifteen years. Reopened in 2002, the carousel is one of three thousand to four thousand wooden carousels carved between 1885 and 1930. Fewer than 150 are still in operation.

In 2003, a reservoir at the southern edge of the park was uncovered and restored. Built in the mid-1800s to collect underground water and provide a water supply for nearby buildings, the reservoir had lain idle for more than a hundred years. A concrete wall surrounding the reservoir was rebuilt, and Victorian-style wrought-iron railings were re-created from historic photos. Replicas of the original antique urns were fabricated, and the pond was stocked with several large rainbow trout.

Though the *Spit and Spat* fountain remained a much-loved feature of the Italian garden, the upper area of the garden suffered great losses over the years, the statuary succumbing to theft or vandalism. In 2005, work was begun to replace the four original statues and the sundial. Marblecast in Salt Lake City, Utah, reconstructed the statues from old photos and postcards. Clay prototypes were made and the statues were cast in a stone aggregate that included marble powder. A replica of the original sundial was constructed by Matthew Hanlon Restorations in New York City. Its inscription, by English poet William Robert Spencer, reads, "Noiseless falls the foot of time, which only treads on flowers." The gardens were rededicated in a public ceremony on July 11, 2007.

One of the oldest existing features in Congress Park consists of a pair of large vases made by Danish artist (Albert) Bertel Thorvaldsen and imported by Dr. John Clarke in 1824. The black and white cast-iron vessels, called *Night and Day*, depict the mythical female likenesses of sunrise and sunset. Although they are now situated near the Canfield Casino, historic photos show that the vases had been in various locations in the park throughout the years, including adjacent to the Victorian arcade entrance on Spring Street.

Congress Park comes alive each spring with a showy display of flowering trees and beds of cheerful tulips planted around many of the landmarks. Once past their prime, the bulbs are removed and replaced with annuals. The city experiments with new varieties each year

The changing face of Congress Park. *Above:* When the *Spirit of Life* fountain was completed in 1914, the Grand Union Hotel formed its backdrop. COURTESY SARATOGA ROOM, SARATOGA LIBRARY. *Center:* The fountain in 2008, after the construction of the Congress Park Centre. *Left:* The Victorian bandstand adjacent to the pond was the site of many summertime concerts in the park. COURTESY SARATOGA ROOM, SARATOGA LIBRARY

to keep things fresh. Improvements to the park, which is listed on the National Register of Historic Places, are ongoing. In 2008, new pathways and benches were installed. The city also began talks of an extensive renovation of the *Spirit of Life* monument, which is in need of significant repairs. These continuing efforts symbolize the commitment by the city to preserve and improve this integral part of Saratoga's past, present, and future. ⚜

The reflecting pool in front of the Hall of Springs is like a mirror on a calm late-summer day. *Opposite:* An urn at the National Museum of Dance, designed by Suzanne Birdsall

Spa Park: A *Place* OF *Renewal*

*S*aratoga's famed mineral springs, which were integral to the city's growth and its reputation as a world-class destination, were often found in clusters. The earliest springs were centered around Congress Spring and to the north at High Rock. A larger cluster of springs was concentrated in an area one mile south of the center of town, in what was known as Geyser Park.

The waters, which people either imbibed or bathed in, gained an international reputation for their reputed curative properties. They were also enjoyed for inducing relaxation and a general sense of well-being. The springs, each with its own unique mineral and gas (carbon dioxide) composition, were used in treating a host of maladies, including skin ailments, arthritis, and heart, circulatory, and digestive conditions.

During the 1890s, gas and bottling plants were constructed in Geyser Park to meet the growing demand for carbonic acid, a key ingredient in carbonated beverages. Massive

amounts of water pumped out of the ground to extract the gas dropped the water table by a hundred feet and severely damaged the aquifer from which the springs flowed.

Quick action was needed to save the springs from total devastation. Community leaders Spencer Trask and state senator Edgar T. Brackett were among those who spearheaded legislation to protect the precious natural resource. In 1908, the Anti-Pumping Act was passed, placing all area springs under state supervision. A state reservation was created to ensure the springs' conservation for generations to come.

The next two decades saw regulated development of the Geyser Park area, which would eventually become part of Saratoga Spa State Park. The Washington Baths were completed in 1920, followed by the adjacent Lincoln Baths in 1930.

Soon after being stricken by polio in 1924 at the age of thirty-nine, Franklin Delano Roosevelt took interest in the potential healing powers of mineral waters. His friend George Foster Peabody (Spencer Trask's business partner) informed Roosevelt of the positive results that polio victims were achieving at Warm Springs in Georgia, where Roosevelt himself would go for therapy. Peabody, a native of Columbus, Georgia, maintained strong ties between his birthplace and his adopted home in upstate New York. While governor of

Left to right: The Lincoln Baths offered patrons various spa treatments. A sculpture depicting Earth is one of the statues flanking the entrance to the Hall of Springs. The National Museum of Dance faces a circular bed landscaped with perennials and annuals.

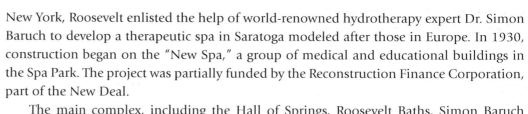

New York, Roosevelt enlisted the help of world-renowned hydrotherapy expert Dr. Simon Baruch to develop a therapeutic spa in Saratoga modeled after those in Europe. In 1930, construction began on the "New Spa," a group of medical and educational buildings in the Spa Park. The project was partially funded by the Reconstruction Finance Corporation, part of the New Deal.

The main complex, including the Hall of Springs, Roosevelt Baths, Simon Baruch Research Laboratory, Gideon Putnam Hotel, and the recreation building, was completed in 1935 and was visited by President Roosevelt that same year. The bathhouses and research laboratory were the basis for medical therapies, both internal and external. The Hall of Springs housed three fountains where patrons could drink the waters. The spas were also available for recreational soaking. The completion of the New Spa helped establish hydrotherapy as a legitimate medicinal treatment.

A mix of Colonial Revival and Beaux Arts architecture, the brick buildings of the New Spa were distinguished by massive columns and wide marble verandas. The complex was designed along a central axis with a large rectangular reflecting pool. The formal European-style landscape consisted of a wide expanse of green lawn punctuated by shade trees and a network of intersecting pathways. Four statues representing the basic elements of earth, wind, fire, and water were planned, but only two were completed due to a lack of funding. The statues of *Earth* and *Water* grace the facade of the Hall of Springs; the facing research laboratory has only empty stone alcoves where the other two statues were meant to be placed.

The spa complex and the area known as Geyser Park were part of 2,500 acres that were incorporated into a state park in 1962. The completion of the Saratoga Performing Arts

Center (SPAC) in 1966 helped establish the city as a top cultural destination. Adjacent to the Hall of Springs, the outdoor venue attracts a wide array of events. Saratoga Spa State Park was designated as a National Historic Landmark in 1987.

The Present-Day Park

The Spa Park offers a multitude of recreational and cultural venues year-round. The bucolic preserve comprises an expansive mix of natural fields and woods seamlessly blended with man-made landscapes. Its open vistas can be enjoyed along miles of hiking trails that wind among the geysers and springs. The park also offers other healthy pursuits: tennis, golf, jogging, biking, picnicking, fishing, and swimming in two public pools. Winter activities include cross-country skiing, ice-skating, and snowshoeing.

Both wild and cultivated flowers are an integral part of the park's ambiance. The formal landscaping is managed by a patchwork of organizations. Plantings at the park entrance, Route 9 medians, toll booths, Victoria and Peerless pools, the Simon Baruch Research Laboratory (now the park's administrative offices and home to the Spa Little Theater), and the Lincoln Baths are maintained by the state. The Hall of Springs, which houses the offices of SPAC and a banquet facility, does its own plantings. The landmark Gideon Putnam Hotel, which manages the Roosevelt Baths, is responsible for the hotel grounds.

A mixed flower border along the front of the Saratoga Automobile Museum, which

opened in 2002 in a former bottling plant, is maintained by volunteers, with materials donated by Sunnyside Gardens. The beds are planted with annual purple fountain grass (*Pennisetum setaceum* 'Rubrum'), impatiens, coleus, and purple millet (*Pennisetum glaucum* 'Purple Majesty'). Perennial alliums, bleeding heart, hosta, rudbeckia, daylilies, and obedient plant (*Physostegia virginiana*) bloom in different seasons. Bold stands of tropical elephant's ear (*Colocasia esculenta*) and castor bean (*Ricinus communis*) add a Victorian flair, keeping the border in scale with the imposing brick and glass facade.

The National Museum of Dance, located in the former Washington Baths, also maintains its own grounds. The only museum in the nation dedicated to professional dance, it was established in 1986. Inductees into its hall of fame include dance legends Fred Astaire, Martha Graham, and Bill Robinson and theater choreographer Bob Fosse.

A large island bed at the front entrance of the Arts and Crafts–style building is planted with perennial English boxwood (*Buxus*), daylilies, and Russian sage (*Perovskia atriplicifolia*), accented with petunias. On either side of the driveway is a columned arcade with large marble urns as focal points. The planters (designed in 2008 by Suzanne Birdsall) are adorned with a bright mix of purple fountain grass, chartreuse potato vines (*Ipomoea batatas* 'Margarita'), purple and gold Million Bells (*Calibrachoa*), and hot pink petunias. Similarly decorated urns and hanging baskets of Boston ferns grace the main entrance.

In its early years, Victoria Pool, the first heated swimming pool in the United States, became a popular hangout for celebrities such as Bing Crosby, Ethel Barrymore, and Jean Harlow. The elegant pool is flanked by a limestone deck and surrounded with classic brick colonnades. The landscaping between the deck and the brick perimeter was redone when the landmark was restored in 2005. The new design incorporates a wide variety of shrubs, trees, and perennials that provide foliage, and flowers from spring until fall. Annuals are mixed in to provide an additional burst of color in summer.

A Showstopping Grand Entrance

One of the park's best-known features is the Avenue of Pines (also called the Pine Promenade), which begins at the main Route 9 entrance to the park. The road was constructed in 1912 to connect Lincoln and Geyser parks. Two rows of eastern white pines, which reach eighty to a hundred feet tall at maturity, were planted on each side of a mile-long stretch of the road. The narrow colonnade evokes the feeling of a majestic cathedral.

In 1999, Julie Stokes, Cheryl Gold, and Stephen McCorkell of the New York Office of Parks and Historic Preservation redesigned the Avenue of Pines entrance, reworking the medians and outlining crescent-shaped flower beds. The following spring, Dan Urkevich planted a mix of perennials, annuals, and shrubs in the new beds. Inspired by historic photos, Urkevich expanded the borders a little more each year, experimenting with different varieties and noting how they responded to where they were planted.

Far left: A planter at the Spa Park administrative offices is a study in foliage color. *Left:* The flower borders at Victoria Pool, impressive even in this undated black and white photo, were inspiration for the spectacular entrance gardens at Spa Park today. COURTESY SARATOGA SPA STATE PARK. *Above:* Tall castor bean plants add a Victorian flair outside the Saratoga Automobile Museum.

The twin borders, each one hundred feet long and nearly twenty feet deep, are situated on a busy road where many locals and summer tourists pass each day. The bloom is timed to reach maximum color during July and August, when the number of racing fans and SPAC patrons reaches its peak. Urkevich wanted to create a garden, he says, "that you could appreciate going by in a car at fifty miles an hour." He anchors the beds with impressive stands of castor bean, elephant's ear, giant sunflowers, and Joe-Pye weed. Bold swaths of other annual and perennial flowers, in hot colors of pink, yellow, orange, and red, create an instant visual impact. White impatiens and other light-hued flowers are interspersed to cast an ethereal glow at twilight, when concertgoers are headed into SPAC for evening performances.

Urkevich has learned by trial and error what will grow best in various light and soil conditions. Though the two borders might look symmetrical from the road at first glance, the southern border is more shaded, and Urkevich adjusts the plantings accordingly, adding more hostas and impatiens. The north border receives more hot afternoon sun, making plants grow taller and sturdier. Across from the entrance, the heavily trafficked Route 9 poses a safety hazard for workers, so the medians are planted with varieties that need little water or fertilizer. Two college students assist Urkevich during the growing season.

In late spring, the orange foxtail lilies *(Eremurus)* put on a spectacular show. The bulbous plants, hardy to USDA Zone 6, are marginal this far north but able to survive with a generous mulch and winter snow cover. The borders become increasingly colorful as other perennials come into bloom, including iris, perennial sunflower, bee balm, sedums, phlox, lamb's-ears *(Stachys)*, daylilies, black-eyed Susan, ribbon grass *(Phalaris)*, and goldenrod. Gaps are filled with spider flower *(Cleome hassleriana)*, African daisies *(Osteospermum)*, dusty miller *(Artemisia)*, blue and red salvias, zinnias, and snapdragons. Urkevich relies heavily on what he refers to as the "workhorses," such as coleus, cockscomb *(Celosia)*, and Supertunias to produce a tapestry of color over a long time with minimum fuss.

Maintaining such lush, healthy plantings is no easy task. The beds are amended with truckloads of compost in spring, and a 14-14-14 timed-release granular fertilizer is worked into the beds before they are planted. During the growing season, Urkevich supplements with a water-soluble fertilizer when the beds are watered so they get an additional boost of nutrients at regular intervals.

When talking about the gardens, Urkevich lights up with enthusiasm. He takes great pride in showing visitors the flowers and answering questions such as how to overwinter the foxtail lilies, or the secret to growing elephant's ear the size of—elephant's ears. Locals take notice of his handiwork, some referring to the spectacular flower borders as simply "Dan's border." In 2007, the gardens were recognized in a citywide beautification contest as a winner in the commercial display category. ❧

The curving mixed borders at the entrance to the Spa Park come into peak bloom in August. *Right:* Annuals add a splash of color at Victoria Pool.

Above: The decorative antique fence at Bill Dorr's Union Avenue garden once graced the grand United States Hotel. *Left:* The Hotel Victoria was smaller than some of the other luxury hotels, but its landscaped courtyard was no less beautiful.

COURTESY SARATOGA ROOM, SARATOGA LIBRARY

Right: The courtyard at the Grand Union Hotel was the place for a leisurely stroll amidst the beautiful landscaping.

Lost Gardens OF *Saratoga*

With the Spa City's resounding booms and disappointing busts, throughout the community's many successes and failures, so came and went many of its gardens. Flowers are integral to Saratoga's past, beginning with the landscaping of Congress Park and its adjacent hotels. The extravagant mansions and estates of the resort city's wealthy and sometimes famous residents were often lavishly landscaped.

The elaborate floral festivals at the turn of the nineteenth century began an era of local horticultural enthusiasm that would sustain the community for decades to come. One can even look back millions of years, when the forces of nature were creating the unique conditions that would produce the city's famed springs. Tiny prehistoric plants in an ancient tropical sea would become fossilized, preserved into a rock reef that became a popular local attraction. For many of these lost landscapes, only pictures, writings, and personal memories remain.

Living Large in Saratoga's Luxury Hotels

An integral part of Saratoga's rise to prominence in the nineteenth century was its grand hotels. During the 1870s, the three largest—Congress Hall, the Union Hotel, and the United States Hotel—could collectively accommodate five thousand guests, more than any other destination in the world. Many of these elaborate resorts were lavishly landscaped with beautiful courtyards and gardens where patrons could stroll, sit, and be entertained by musical groups and theater productions. These outdoor spaces served an important social function for visiting guests.

The Grand Union Hotel

Gideon Putnam's original boarding house was expanded and renamed Union Hall. After it was sold in 1864 to the Leland brothers, Warren and Charles, who were well-known hotel entrepreneurs, they expanded the resort, naming it the Union Hotel. The expansive building across from Congress Park had more than seven hundred rooms that could accommodate fifteen hundred guests. Musical groups entertained guests in the landscaped courtyard.

The hotel was purchased by Alexander Stewart, who refurbished and reopened the resort in 1874 as the Grand Union Hotel. A prominent feature of the five-story building was its spacious courtyard shaded by stately elm trees. Guests could take a leisurely stroll along gently curving pathways and sit on the occasional wooden bench to enjoy the surroundings. The paths wound along formal green lawns and brightly colored flower beds. The centerpiece of the courtyard was a large classical fountain and pool. Star-shaped beds, which were popular during the Victorian era, were planted with canna lilies and brightly colored annuals. Tropical palms lent a feeling of luxury.

Afternoon garden parties were held for the guests' children on a decorated platform. Other galas were held for adult guests in the evenings. The hotel also hosted outdoor Shakespearean performances in the backdrop of the landscaped courtyard.

With the advent of the automobile, tourists were no longer bound to staying in one place for long periods of time. The large hotels fell out of favor, and it became too expensive to update the massive buildings. The Grand Union Hotel was finally razed in 1952–53. Before it was demolished, though, many of its furnishings were sold in a public auction, and some of Saratoga's longtime residents still own a piece of this historic structure.

The United States Hotel

Saratoga's other large hotel, the United States, was renowned for its picturesque courtyard and magnificent gardens. The original hotel was erected in 1823 and burned in 1865. It was rebuilt on the same site on a scale to rival that of the Grand Union. The new hotel, with nine hundred rooms, could accommodate two thousand guests. The imposing five-story brick and stone building, completed and reopened in 1874, had a two-story colonnade with a 232-foot-long piazza facing the street where guests could gather and socialize. Large circular planting beds between the veranda and the sidewalk held trailing vines and large stands of tropical palms.

The courtyard inside the perimeter of the hotel was landscaped with a wide expanse of green lawn and neat symmetrical paths. Elm trees, their trunks a lush green with climbing ivy, were planted in rows along the hotel's promenade and the central walk. A multitiered cast-iron fountain surrounded by a round pool was one of several large ornamental features. The courtyard glowed at night, when it was softly illuminated with colored lights and lanterns.

The large hotel also succumbed to the realities of the twentieth century, seized by the city in 1943 for nonpayment of property taxes. The lavish furnishings were sold and the building was razed in 1946.

Hotel Victoria

The gardens at Hotel Victoria were more modest in scale than those of the larger hotels, but they were no less bucolic. A round pool with a fountain at the center was rimmed with tall shade trees, and adjacent wooden benches offered a place to sit. Colorful blooming shrubs were planted around the periphery, and small round beds set in the formal lawn were planted with bright annuals. Flower boxes decorated the picket fence–style railing along a narrow porch that ran the length of the first story. The occasional small urn completed the embellishments.

The demise of Saratoga's great hotels represents the end of an opulent era. The Adelphi Hotel (www.adelphihotel.com) on Broadway, which once accommodated two hundred guests, is the last of the old hotels remaining.

A Timeless Landscape

With Saratoga's unique geology, combined with the city's long affiliation with flowers and gardening, it seems fitting that there would be a nearby ancient "garden" fossilized in rock. The Petrified Sea Gardens, located several miles west of downtown Saratoga off Route 29, were part of an ocean reef formed 500 million years ago when

the area was at the edge of a warm tropical sea. As the tide lapped the shore, layers of stromatolites built up in domed formations. They were later polished by glaciers, exposing the fossils in cross sections.

Stromatolites were created from microscopic organisms known as blue-green algae; they are the oldest known preserved life forms, going back some three billion years. The primitive flora were thought to be a major producer of the earth's oxygen and the oldest known plants to produce chlorophyll. Two other fossilized life forms unique to the site are two types of sea bugs, one named *Saratogia calcifera* in honor of the city. A piece of stromatolite from the grounds, shaped like a human face, was named Old Man Saratoga and was once featured in *Ripley's Believe It or Not*.

The fossilized site was discovered and identified by Robert R. Ritchie in 1923, allegedly after a cow grazing in a pasture fell into a crevice hidden under a layer of soil and

Top: At the Grand Union Hotel, paths led strollers past fountains and star-shaped flower beds. *Bottom:* The courtyard at the United States Hotel was known for its ivy-covered elms and multi-tiered fountains. *Right:* The rock gardens at the Petrified Sea Gardens were landscaped by Robert A. Ritchie and his wife, who opened the fossil formation as a tourist attraction in the 1930s. ALL COURTESY SARATOGA ROOM, SARATOGA LIBRARY

grass. Ritchie, a Scottish immigrant stonemason, and his brother were best known for building the Katrina Trask staircase in Congress Park. The fossilized reef and other unique stone formations were eventually uncovered, and the thirty-acre site was opened to the

public in 1933. Rock gardens and an armillary garden on the grounds were beautifully landscaped with flowers, shrubs, and vines. Visitors could actually walk across the one-acre fossilized reef, which is punctuated by deep crevasses that eroded years ago and exposed the internal structure of the formation.

Called "living fossils," a dawn redwood (*Metasequoia glyptostroboides*) and a gingko (*G. biloba*) were planted to illustrate two examples of ancient trees once thought to be extinct. An impressive white pine *(Pinus strobus)*, growing here since 1700, was dubbed the Iroquois pine for its proximity to an old Indian trail.

Ritchie built a stone gate at the entrance to the Petrified Sea Gardens and a fireplace in the main building made from loosened fossils. Also on the grounds are a stone lion, an Indian medicine wheel, a labyrinth, a "time garden," and a lily pond. A Buddha wishing well and a fossilized rock garden were landscaped by Ritchie and his wife, Elizabeth, who lived for a time on the property. Some areas were landscaped with flowers, shrubs, and vines, and the rock gardens were lush with naturalized daffodils, iris, and other colorful flowers.

WALK IN CHAUNCEY OLCOTT'S GARDENS, SARATOGA SPRINGS, N. Y.

The Petrified Sea Gardens were designated a National Natural Landmark in 1967 and a National Historic Landmark in 1999. The property, owned by the adjacent D. A. Collins Companies, allowed the nonprofit Friends of Petrified Sea Gardens to keep the grounds open to the public. The site was closed in 2006 due to severe storm damage. The main building, which housed the fireplace, succumbed to the elements and was subsequently torn down. Plans are under way to clean up the site, with the hopes that it can be reopened to the public at a future date.

Saratoga's Irish Rose

The moniker of one of Saratoga's most famous residents isn't exactly a household name, but many of the songs he wrote are instantly recognized across the world. Chancellor John "Chauncey" Olcott, who spent thirty summers in the Spa City, was best known for composing the classic song "My Wild Irish Rose" and writing the lyrics to the timeless ballad "When Irish Eyes Are Smiling." Born to Irish immigrant parents in Buffalo, New York, in 1860, Olcott embraced his heritage and knew at an early age that he wanted to become a singer.

His soaring tenor voice caught the attention of famed singer-actress Lillian Russell, who was also known to enjoy Saratoga's high life. She cast him as the leading man in the

Far left: An armillary is one remnant from the original Petrified Sea Gardens. *Center, top to bottom:* Enclosed gardens and flower-lined paths at the beautifully landscaped grounds of Chauncey Olcott's Inniscara estate. *Above:* A quaint thatched cottage and at Inniscara. HISTORIC PHOTOS COURTESY SARATOGA ROOM, SARATOGA LIBRARY

operetta *Pepita,* launching his career on Broadway. Olcott would go on to perform internationally as a singer and comedic opera performer.

In 1897, Olcott married Rita O'Donovan, a writer and occasional playwright. She wrote her husband's biography, *Song in His Heart,* where she recounted the couple's search for a summer home, a quiet place in the country set among apple trees. Their journey led them back to Saratoga, where they had spent their honeymoon. After a fruitless search for just the right house, they discovered and purchased a two-acre parcel, the site of an abandoned apple orchard at the edge of town.

In 1903, they built a two-story Dutch Colonial home in the "Irish style," with a spacious porch that looked out onto the back of the property rather than the street. Olcott named the property Inniscara for a town in County Cork, Ireland, where he and Rita spent time as newlyweds. The home also was referred to as "The Candy House" by some of the neighbors.

Olcott and his wife created an elaborate landscape on their Clinton Street property, with some of the most lavish and extensive gardens to be found in the Spa City. The gardens were famously immortalized in an immensely popular series of early-1900s colorized postcards. The landscape's design was incorporated into the original plans of the house, with the main walkways in harmony with the home's architecture.

The flower beds were laid out along perpendicular pathways with a central axis in a classic formal European style. The boisterous proliferation of colorful blooms was reminiscent of the older gardens found throughout the British Isles. A long walkway that stretched along the porch was lined on one side with rosebushes. Olcott was especially fond of gardening and was often found tending his roses. A semicircular metal hoop rose arbor greeted visitors at the porch entrance. Tall shade trees and shrubs provided a lush backdrop to the flower borders.

The backyard gardens were enclosed by a neatly clipped waist-high hedge, anchored by taller columnar evergreens. Inside the hedge was a series of smaller garden rooms connected by narrow footpaths. At the central axis was an enchanting wishing well, reminiscent of those found in children's picture books. From here, a long path extended through a series of rectangular metal arbors. Allées of trees on either side of the path were flanked by wide expanses of lush green lawns. At the end of the path was a rose garden with a thirty-foot-long vine-covered arbor and the gardener's cottage. For recreation, handball and tennis courts were constructed near the horse stables on an adjacent property.

One of the most charming features of the garden was the tiny ornamental cottage that Rita had constructed as a surprise for her husband. With an authentic thatched roof, the quaint structure looked like something transplanted from an Irish country scene. The roof of an adjacent birdhouse set atop a high pole was also whimsically thatched.

The Olcotts, who loved to entertain, hosted grand parties at their estate, inviting notable guests such as President Grover Cleveland, Sam Riddle (owner of the thoroughbred Man o' War), conductor-composer Fritz Kreisler, future president Franklin D. Roosevelt, and actor-producer Henry Miller. The gardens were said to have been lit up at night like a fairyland as guests drifted along the pathways, breathing in the warm night air perfumed with the sweet scent of roses. Olcott loved horse racing as much as anything else he cherished of Saratoga, and spent most August afternoons at the racetrack.

As all gardens do, the Olcott garden underwent changes over the years. Some of the arbors and trellises were moved or torn down, and plants were replaced. The thatched roof on the cottage was replaced with traditional shingles. During World War II, the Olcott family planted a large victory garden at the back of the property.

Saratoga's famed Irish tenor passed away in 1932—appropriately, on St. Patrick's Day. His funeral, held at St. Patrick's Cathedral in New York City, was attended by throngs of mourners. The greenery on his casket was brought down from Inniscara, and some of the plants from his beloved estate were transplanted to his grave site.

After Olcott's death, his wife continued to spend part of the year in Saratoga. Olcott's grandson and namesake, Chauncey Olcott Johnstone, recalls spending summers at Inniscara as a child. The gardens were a favorite place for him and his sister to play, the many garden rooms providing secret hiding places to explore. The "Thatch," as the family referred to the little cottage, was sometimes used as a playhouse. Curious passersby would come by the house to look because they heard that someone famous had lived there. The children would

Flower-bedecked horse-drawn carriages and bicycle brigades were mainstays of the early Floral Fête parades.

ALL COURTESY SARATOGA ROOM, SARATOGA LIBRARY

throw open the gate to let them in, and the visitors would inevitably toss money into the wishing well. As soon as they left, Johnstone and his sister would fish out the change.

Johnstone also recalls his mother, Janet Olcott Johnstone (a well-regarded pianist in her own right), helping out with Japanese beetle control in the rose garden. Apparently, stronger measures were thought necessary back then beyond the soap and water remedy commonly used today: Johnstone's mother would tote a brush and a coffee can filled with kerosene through the rose garden, where she whisked each bug from the plants into the tin, to its instant demise.

Rita Olcott passed away in 1949, and Inniscara was sold to Mary Levingston, who willed it to Skidmore College in 1975. The school used the property for staff housing. In the 1980s it was sold to Bill and Alyce Stevens, horse breeders and the owners of Harry M. Stevens, Inc., one of the nation's earliest concessionaires. By 1900, the company was selling food and drinks at many of the major league ballparks and racetracks around the country, including the Saratoga Race Course. Its founder, Harry M. Stevens, is widely credited with inventing America's favorite snack, the hot dog.

By the time Bill and Alyce Stevens arrived at Inniscara, which was listed on the National Register of Historic Places, the estate had lost most of the original landscaping, but Alyce, an avid gardener, created new flower beds of her own. Some of the original shrubs and orchard trees, such as lilacs, cherries, pears, and apples, had survived. In 1999, Bill and Alyce opened their estate to the public for the annual Soroptimist garden tour. Alyce passed away in 2006, and Bill fell into ill health; the estate was sold in 2008.

The spirit of Inniscara lives on in Olcott's immortal compositions, including the operetta *Sweet Inniscara*, which he wrote in honor of his beloved home. Though his gardens are now gone, the Spa City that he loved was made richer for his bigger-than-life presence.

Floral Fêtes of the Victorian Era

The 1890s represented a crossroads in the history of Saratoga Springs. Although many businesses and tourism still flourished, the village's renown as a haven for gambling and horse racing was the subject of increasing controversy among reformists. Community leaders were forced to reevaluate the future direction of the city and contemplate various solutions.

At a public meeting in the fall of 1893, Franklin Webster Smith presented his ideas on how to improve the city's image. Smith was best known for his House of Pansa on Broadway, a museum-quality replica of an AD 79 Pompeian villa. One of his suggestions was that the city hold a floral festival, complete with a grand parade and ball. Reaction was mixed, but Smith was undeterred. The following spring, he planted a one-third-acre wildflower meadow adjacent to the newly constructed Convention Hall. That display was received with great public enthusiasm, and the idea of a festival was revived.

The first Annual Floral Fête and Battle of Flowers, held on September 4, 1894, was a resounding success. A majestic parade was staged along a 1.25-mile route that extended from the Broadway entrance of Congress Park to Woodlawn Park (now the Skidmore

College campus). Between twenty-five and thirty-five thousand spectators lined the sidewalks, hotel piazzas, and balconies to watch a procession of bicycles and horse-drawn carriages and floats, all lavishly festooned with gaily colored blooms. The piazzas and balconies of Congress Hall and the United States and Grand Union hotels each held a thousand people, according to one estimate. The Battle of Flowers, originating from European festivals such as in Nice, France, referred to the practice of spectators and participants taking flowers "to be thrown as missiles" at one another during the parade, or after the floral floats were dismantled.

Flowers from the meadow beside the Convention Hall were used to adorn the parade vehicles. Other blooms brought in from the surrounding countryside included goldenrod, asters, daisies, and Queen Anne's lace, along with mountain ash berries, and brightly colored autumn leaves. Cultivated hydrangeas, roses, marigolds, sunflowers, phlox, and gladioli were cut from local gardens. Boughs of cedar, hemlock, and pine provided soft green backdrops.

Several brigades of decorated bicycles led the procession, followed by carriages proceeding in order of the importance of their passengers. Notable community leaders, out-of-town guests, and socialites went first. Every inch of the carriages, from the body, top, and running gear to the wheel spokes, was covered in flowers. The horses were decorated with plumes of goldenrod, and yards of satin ribbon lined the harnesses. The vehicles included an array of carts, buckboards, cabriolets, and landaus. Male passengers were decked with flower-trimmed coats and hats, and the ladies carried parasols adorned with flowers and ferns.

More than two dozen floats with themes of art, history, or mythology were sponsored by local businesses and school and church groups. The lead float, a Roman chariot with the likeness of the goddesses Pomona (fruits) and Flora (flowers) and the god Asclepius (medicinal herbs), was drawn by four oxen. The Congress Hall float, which depicted the discovery of High Rock Spring by Native Americans, carried a realistic replica of the rock formation. Other floats were decked out with local produce such as cornstalks, oat straw, fruits, colorful ears of corn, and crabapples.

Some floats featured musical entertainment, including one with an Italian orchestra and a harpist. The Bethesda Sunday School float transported a chorus of fifty children singing songs such as "God Bless Our Native Land." Another Sunday school float carried a musical ensemble consisting of a children's choir, a piano, two trumpets, and three violins.

A grand floral ball held at Convention Hall that evening was attended by three thousand guests and lasted well into the night. The auditorium was decorated with Japanese lanterns and evergreen garlands strung from the balcony. A brass band and an orchestra performed on the stage, which was decorated to resemble a fairy bower. The orchestra played Tchaikovsky's "Waltz of the Flowers," as well as the accompaniment to special dance performances.

The festival's immense popularity posed logistical problems the following year, when an estimated fifty thousand spectators poured into the village. Even so, not all of the would-be spectators made it into town. An article in the *New York Times* dated September

8, 1895, remarked, "More people would have been in (Saratoga) on Thursday if the transportation companies had anticipated the rush and equipped their roads with sufficient cars to meet the sudden demand. The simple fact was that there were not enough cars to bring the people here, and it was a source of much disappointment to those who were left behind at many of the stations within a radius of fifty miles." The 1895 parade consisted of sixty carriages, thirty-five floats, live music, and a cavalcade of bicyclists, all adorned with flowers. The floral ball in Convention Hall that evening was attended by seven thousand people.

By the festival's third year, in 1896, the number of spectators had grown to an estimated one hundred thousand. A special feature of that year's parade was a two-thousand-strong bicycle brigade, led by the Olympic Bicycle Band. The two-wheeled vehicles had became a popular mode of transportation during the Victorian era, and were widely embraced by Saratogians. Some of the single and tandem bikes were tied together into units that pulled carriages or were part of their own floats.

Saratoga's floral fête grew in scope and grandeur to rival the Pasadena (California) Tournament of Roses parade. As the crowds grew, so did the number, size, and splendor of the parade entries. In 1897, one ton each of asters, roses, and gladioli were used to decorate the floats, carriages, and bicycles. Though most floats were pulled by horses, some were moved by oxen, and a few of the smaller children's carts were drawn by goats or ponies.

By 1900, the festival was held over several days and included a polo match in addition to the ball and parade. A fireworks display at the thoroughbred racetrack was introduced by a musical overture and an artillery salute. The event consisted of an elaborate series of stationary lighted displays in floral and other themes that were punctuated by bursts of fireworks exploding overhead—fourteen separate displays in all. Spectators pressed against the trackside railing when the first fireworks shot into the air, shouting, "They're off!" in jovial reference to the send-off normally given to racehorses as they lunged from the starting gate.

The annual floral fête was discontinued after 1902 because of the expense and difficulty of accommodating the large crowds. The event was briefly revived for one year, in 1924, when the daylong festivities included a two-mile procession featuring half a million blooms, followed by a floral ball at the Convention Hall. The most notable difference between this and the earlier events was the prominence of decorated automobiles.

Though the floral fêtes are now relegated to a past chapter of Saratoga's history, the city's love affair with flowers continues today. ⚜

Clockwise from top left: Cars were part of the 1924 Floral Fête. Note the daisy hubcaps and the dragonflies on the front of this 1908 Oldsmobile touring car. The postcard image demonstrates how some floats were astonishing in their size and detail. Music was the theme of the horse-drawn float at bottom. ALL COURTESY SARATOGA ROOM, SARATOGA LIBRARY

The city maintains plantings and hanging baskets along Broadway.

A *Citywide Beautification*

During the 1970s and 1980s, the city of Saratoga Springs experienced a gradual renaissance. Local government officials and residents began to fully realize the importance of historic preservation, and a civic pride began to spread. Congress Park was revitalized with extensive improvements, including the restoration of its monuments and the construction of a new pavilion over Congress Spring. Mansions that had fallen into disrepair or been divided into multifamily dwellings were bought by appreciative owners and lovingly restored to their former elegance. Small businesses reinvested in vacant storefronts, revitalizing the downtown area with specialty shops, fine restaurants, and stylish boutiques.

The spirit of hope and rebirth extended to improvements in the city's landscape. The newly formed Saratoga Springs Preservation Foundation obtained a grant to assist local merchants in planting flowers around their storefronts. Funding and resources were authorized by the city government to upgrade landscaping. Trees, shrubs, and flowers were planted in Congress Park and other public spots.

In 1979, local elementary schoolteacher James Gapczynski was hired for the summer to become the chief of the Saratoga Springs Flower Power program. City officials noticed his beautifully landscaped yard on Union Avenue and approached him about duplicating his efforts in the medians across from the thoroughbred race course. That first year, five hundred annuals were planted in island beds along Union Avenue between East and

Nelson Avenues. The colorful plantings were extremely popular, and the program was expanded the following year to include Congress Park and the downtown area.

By 1990, Gapczynski was in charge of planting fifty thousand flowers, assisted by a crew of nineteen high school and college students. In addition to the Union Avenue medians, they tended beds around the statuary at Congress Park and added flower boxes, curbside plantings, and hanging baskets along the business district on Broadway. Urns and pots brimming with cheerful annuals were placed around City Hall. The city's venerable mineral springs, including Hathorn and Old Red springs, were decorated. An assortment of petunias, begonias, impatiens, coleus, and marigolds brought a welcome burst of color across the city.

The stunning floral displays were noticed by visitors and locals alike, and area residents would often stop the flower crew to ask advice for their own yards. Local nurseries saw a surge in retail sales as customers sought to re-create similar plantings. Neighborhood porches, yards, and curbsides became increasingly adorned with hanging baskets, perennial borders, and annual plantings. Lawn jockeys and Victorian urns were popular lawn decorations, becoming part of the city's unique identity.

During the first few years of the Flower Power program, workers hauled buckets of water by hand to the flower beds. This limited the ability to expand the program, so an out-of-service fire engine was employed to transport and dispense water to the plants. The vintage 1952 Mack pumper truck, emblazoned with the words "Flower Power," became a familiar sight on city streets.

Though Gapczynski left the program in 1990, one of his lasting contributions was the crescent-shaped bed at the intersection of Union Avenue and Circular Street. Dubbed the "message board" by the city's crew, the raised bed was planted with flowers to spell out the word *Saratoga*.

Later, the day's date would also be spelled out in annual begonias, dusty miller, or petunias. Every day around 6 a.m., city workers would update the display, rearranging the flower pots in a carefully orchestrated method. The letters and numbers for each month and day were pre-assembled, packed into nursery flats, and stored in greenhouses until needed. The original pressure-treated timber planting bed was refurbished with a stone structure. In 2009 the display was redesigned with a small waterfall as the centerpiece and the tradition of spelling out the date with plants was discontinued.

Today, the city continues planting the original areas, as well as beds at the visitor center across from Congress Park; the Saratoga County Arts Council, at Broadway and Spring Street; and welcome signs at the city border. A long median at the intersection of Routes 9N and 50 is known to the city crew as "Fire Island" because of the amount of heat it retains from the surrounding asphalt. The crew takes advantage of the warm microclimate, planting heat-loving cockscomb or scarlet sage *(Salvia splendens)* around stands of dwarf canna lilies.

If the city's budget is any indication, Saratoga Springs takes its blooms seriously. In 1989, $9,000 was allotted to blanket the city with colorful flowers; by 2008, the budget had grown to $20,000. The Downtown Business Association contributes another $6,000 for storefront plantings along Broadway.

Left: Even the signs along Broadway are decorated with flower boxes. *Above, left and right:* The date on the "message board" at the edge of Congress Park used to be changed daily. When the planting was redesigned in 2008, the tradition of changing the date was discontinued.

Behind the Scenes

The city begins planning for the next season months before the first petunia goes into the ground. In January, Rob Wheelock, who heads the city's beautification crew, and deputy public works commissioner Pat Design begin discussing the upcoming season, evaluating what worked the previous year and what could be improved. Flower crew workers offer additional input. A list is made of flower varieties and quantities needed, and local nurseries are invited to submit a bid. For many years, the annuals were grown to specification at Dehn's Flowers. From 2007 to 2009, the bid was awarded to Sunnyside Gardens.

Petunia cuttings are ordered in February and shipped from Guatemala or Nicaragua. They are planted in soil medium and placed on heated tables until the cuttings are rooted. Most annuals, including impatiens, are grown from seed in on-site greenhouses. New canna bulbs, widely used in the city's landscaping, are reordered each spring because the cost of saving the bulbs from year to year is not cost-effective. The public is invited to dig up the spent bulbs at the end of the season so they don't go to waste.

Hanging baskets along Broadway and at the farmers' market were formerly planted with potato vine, verbena, bacopa, Million Bells, and petunias. More recent baskets have been planted with Wave petunias, which can grow to three to four feet in diameter, making them a good choice as a ground cover or in baskets. They bloom over a long time and don't need to be pinched back, as do older petunia varieties.

Specialty beds, which contain a broader palette of plants, are planted in medians along Union Avenue, the entrance borders at Congress Park, and a few other select locations. A typical design might include blue salvia, marigolds, zinnias, dusty miller, and canna lilies.

The tropical hibiscus displayed in Congress Park are overwintered in heated greenhouses. The most impressive of these are two specimens kept in large ceramic pots, their thick trunks trained into braids. The twin plants, more than twenty years old, stand sentinel at the Spring Street entrance near the carousel.

The first baskets are hung in mid-May, around Mother's Day, and inground planting starts near Memorial Day, when all danger of frost is past. The process can take four weeks. By late June, some sixty thousand plants, half of them impatiens, have found their summer home in curbside beds, island plantings, flower boxes, and baskets hung on street lamps and posts.

The city relies heavily on impatiens, as they hold up well in pedestrian areas, bloom over a long period, and don't need to be pinched back. The annual bedding plants tolerate

Left and center: The city maintains the plantings at Hathorn Spring #1 and outside City Hall. The horse sculpture was painted by staff and students at Living Resources. *Right:* Plantings at the front of the Saratoga Springs Visitor Center, once a trolley station, are maintained by the city, but a welcome garden at the side of the historic building is tended by the Heritage Garden Club.

a wide range of light conditions, from sun to full shade. Their height (twelve to eighteen inches) and spreading habit make them a good choice for curbside spots where foot traffic is heavy. Impatiens varieties vary from year to year; as many as two dozen different colors have been grown. In 2009, four different mixes of impatiens in fifteen colors were used in the business district. Nearly fifteen thousand impatiens are planted on Broadway alone.

The city's floral crew increases from twelve to seventeen during peak season. They water the flowers early each morning with four tanker trucks that pump 3,150 gallons of water per day. A water-soluble fertilizer is applied to jump-start the plant growth, then adjusted to a low but steady dose, then increased again in midsummer to stimulate a new growth spurt. By late August, the plants are allowed to wane.

Saratoga Springs has received national recognition for its beautification efforts. In 2007, Thomas McTygue, then commissioner of public works, and Ned Chapman, owner of Sunnyside Gardens, entered the city in a nationwide competition sponsored by the America in Bloom program and won first prize in the floral displays category, which included judging of city plantings as well as business and residential gardens. The success of the Flower Power program and support from the community make the city of Saratoga Springs a winner each and every year. ❧

Merchants Who Mean Business

The city's Flower Power program has spurred many downtown businesses to beautify their own storefronts. Summer patrons are treated to nearly endless displays of flowers.

Right: The sculpture amidst the plantings at the Olde Bryan Inn was painted by well-known equestrian artist Frankie Flores.

Below: The armillary sphere behind the Adirondack Trust Company is a tribute to Saratogian Charles Dow, who first proposed the idea of standardized time zones.

Center top: The Granite Palace Plaza boasts some of the most spectacular plantings on Broadway.

Center bottom: On Maple Avenue, Hidden Gardens has bold plantings and even bolder statuary on display.

Left: Hanging baskets and window boxes adorn a Church Street building.

Below: Lush plantings and a classic fountain grace the grounds of the aptly named Hilton Garden Inn.

And...
They're Off!

*I*n late July, Saratoga Springs is filled with excitement as the thoroughbred racing season begins. The local population of twenty-eight thousand year-round residents swells to include thousands more racing personnel, part-time residents, and tourists. Restaurants and B and Bs, their properties adorned with flowering baskets and decorative urns, fill up with out-of-town tourists. Hotels with classic fountains and planted parking strips post "no vacancy" signs. Seasonal homes are opened, prepared, and landscaped for the trainers, jockeys, and horse owners who live here in summer. Peak attendance for the meet in recent years has reached more than a million spectators.

The Saratoga Race Course, established in 1864, is the oldest continuously operating horse-racing track in the country, and widely regarded as the most scenic. In 1999, *Sports Illustrated* magazine named it one of the top ten sporting venues in the world. Some of the

Left: A horse and jockey parade along the flower-lined paddock at the Saratoga Race Course before the start of a race. *Above:* The lattice shade house behind Peggy Steinman's home dates back to 1800.

greatest equines have run here, including Man o' War and Triple Crown winners Affirmed, War Admiral, Gallant Fox, and Secretariat.

The first meet was organized in 1863 by a group of men that included John Morrissey (owner of the Canfield Casino), William Travers, and Commodore Vanderbilt. The event, held at "Horse Haven," which is now part of the Oklahoma training track, was a huge success, and the newly formed racing association quickly expanded the event the following summer to its present location across the street. The first Travers race was held that year and is now the oldest stakes race for three-year-olds in America.

Saratoga's thoroughbred track is more infamously known as the "Graveyard of Favorites." In 1919, Man o' War suffered his only loss out of twenty-one starts in Saratoga's Sanford Memorial to the aptly named horse Upset. One of the most notorious losses in racing history was endured by Triple Crown winner Gallant Fox, who succumbed to 100-1 long shot Jim Dandy in the 1930 Travers Stakes. The jinx continued into the 1970s, with Triple Crown winner Secretariat losing by a length to Onion in the Whitney Stakes.

The affinity that thousands of race goers feel toward this historically significant venue defies easy explanation. Some of it is surely based on nostalgia. In 1892, the present-day grandstand was built, and other major improvements were made to the grounds. The imposing Queen Anne–style structure, with its dramatic sweeping rooflines, looks much the same as it did during the high Victorian era. The two ovals and the Oklahoma training track, along with the landscaped paddocks, barns, and outbuildings that make up the 350-acre complex, hearken back to a kinder and gentler era.

Veteran race goers from all walks of life have their favorite spots to watch the races. The reserved boxes, where seating is at a premium, adhere to a dress code of sport coats for men and dresses or pantsuits for women. Other dining areas, suites, and outdoor sections have their own standards of dress. The majority of spectators, attired casually in shorts and T-shirts, gravitate to the backyard (the area behind the grandstand), the rows of benches in front of the grandstand, the shaded paddock, or the umbrella-studded picnic tables at the top of the stretch. In a long-standing tradition, attendees are allowed to bring picnic spreads (though not in the grandstand or clubhouse), reserving their preferred spot on the honor system by leaving a racing program, cooler, or portable chairs. Special events include backstretch tours and a trackside breakfast, where spectators can enjoy the early-morning workouts. Giveaway days, where sixty thousand free items are made available to track attendees, are especially popular. Items have included tote bags, caps, T-shirts, umbrellas, stadium seats, blankets and bobble-head figures of famous jockeys and trainers. Collectors known as "spinners" re-enter the turnstiles multiple times, selling the resulting bounty on eBay or gifting the items to friends and relatives.

The Racing Set Arrives

Many local homes, including some of the city's grandest mansions, are occupied by horse owners, jockeys, and trainers for the six-week racing season. The thoroughbred meet is a gay whirlwind of daytime races and nighttime parties. The phone starts to ring at Dehn's Flowers in June as longtime customers call to place their orders for seasonal landscaping. They spare no expense in decorating their properties with flowers for the short time they are in town.

One such client is Peggy Steinman, whose Colonial-style mansion sits across from the Oklahoma training track. The heiress of Lancaster Newspapers in Pennsylvania, and known in horse circles as the "First Lady of Steeplechase," Steinman has owned some impressive jumpers, including her favorite horse, Colstar, who won more than one million dollars in purses during his career. Steinman, a no-nonsense woman with a beehive hairdo and Southern charm, is known to host an occasional party at her summertime home, the grounds suitably decorated with flowers and statuary.

Clockwise from top left: The plantings at Peggy Steinman's imposing Greek Revival–style house pick up her stable's colors of pink and kelly green. Megaphones from Saratoga Race Track's old public address system were turned into planters. Houses on Nelson Avenue, across from the track, are gaily decorated with flowers for the racing season.

In July, a crew from Dehn's Flowers delivers a truckload of impatiens and other bedding plants to Steinman's home. Her own staff plants the flower beds along the house and in back. The landscape is transformed nearly overnight with beds brimming with annuals. Hanging baskets, topiaries, and statuary grace the front porch. The plantings and decorations are all done in shades of pink and kelly green, Steinman's stable colors.

Behind the stately home stands one of the city's oldest structures, a wooden gazebo/shade house constructed around 1800. It has classic columns and Chinese Chippendale lattice, with a seating bench and a graceful soaring roof (shown on page 57). The shelter originally stood on the property of Abram (or Abraham) Markoe a few blocks from Independence Hall in Philadelphia. Captain Markoe was a cavalryman who designed one of America's earliest flags. The gazebo was later moved by barge to the port city of Burlington, New Jersey, where it was transported by road to Clover Hill, the home of Samuel and Elizabeth Baynton Markoe Hazelhurst in Mount Holly.

In 1947, the Hazelhursts' great-grandson, Richard Ashhurst, conferred the gazebo to Walter M. Jeffords, who moved it to Hunting Hill, his estate located south of Philadelphia. Many members of the Jeffords family were well known for horse racing and were related by marriage to Samuel D. Riddle, owner of Man o' War. The gazebo was then moved to the Jeffords family's seasonal home in Saratoga, an elegant mansion on North Broadway.

Steinman, who was a close friend of the Jeffords family, had the gazebo moved to her property in 2004 after the Jeffords home was sold. The garden structure is in remarkable shape given its age and the likely various restorations over its long past.

Left and above: Denise and David Herman's home, carriage house, and rental cottage all brim with summer color. *Right:* A lawn jockey makes a focal point in the Hermans' garden.

The Racing Season

There are two kinds of Saratoga residents: those who relish the excitement and glitz of the racing season, and those who dread the crowds, noise, and boisterous revelry. Some of the latter leave town, renting out their homes for the duration of the meet, a tradition that goes back to Saratoga's Victorian heyday. Those who live adjacent to the track capitalize on their home's proximity. Back-, side, and front yards are temporarily transformed into private parking lots for track goers; on race days, these residents are found at curbside, flagging down potential customers.

One of these seasonal parking lots is located on Nelson Avenue, across from the racetrack's clubhouse turn. Denise Herman, a marathon runner and physical education teacher at Saratoga Springs High School, relishes the excitement and bustle of the track. On race days, Herman crams dozens of cars on the large grassy area in back of her three adjacent homes, one her residence and the other two rentals. The modest Victorian-style cottages were built around 1900 to accommodate summertime visitors. The unheated structures were eventually converted to year-round residences.

The two-story wood frame houses are hard to miss. Herman enjoys dressing up the front yards and porches with plenty of flowers and decorations. Because the space is small, she plants mostly annuals for season-long color. Each porch is crammed with flower boxes and hanging baskets dripping with begonias, miniature dahlias, impatiens, angelonia (*A. angustifolia*), fairy fan-flower (*Scaevola*), blue ageratum, and ivy geraniums (*Pelargonium peltatum*). Deep purple and bright chartreuse potato vines offer contrasting foliage. The porches are also decorated with gaily colored horse banners, posters, and wicker furniture. Small planting beds just in front of each porch hold an eclectic mix of evergreens, perennials, and annuals. Lawn jockeys, one in front of each house, hold flower baskets while appearing to wave at passersby.

A carriage house in back was renovated in 2002. Perennial plantings of black-eyed Susan and Russian sage in complementary colors of purple and gold soften the foundation. The side of the building is adorned with iron-framed window planters and hanging baskets.

Herman doesn't have far to look for her healthy-looking plants. Her husband's sister owns West Shaker Farm in Colonie. Herman makes the trek there around Memorial Day to load up on a wide assortment of annuals in bright hues of purple, orange, and pink.

The spectacular displays look lush and colorful all summer long. Herman waters the flowers daily and applies a weekly dose of Miracle-Gro water-soluble fertilizer at regular strength but more frequently than recommended. Because the plants are watered so often, nutrients leach from the soil more quickly, so the flowers can tolerate a higher dose.

The exuberant flower plantings have become a fixture that racing patrons look forward to each year. Herman finds the gardens to be a lot of work, but regular compliments from passersby make it all worth it.

A Yearling Tradition

One of the highlights of the racing season is the yearling auction held at the Fasig-Tipton grounds on East and Madison avenues. The auction company founded by William B. Fasig and Edward A. Tipton expanded their operations to Saratoga in 1917. Some of the world's top thoroughbreds have changed hands in Saratoga, with buyers risking huge sums on the chance to own a winning horse. Man o' War, who was purchased on the track grounds in 1918 for $5,000, would go on to become one of the greatest racehorses of all time.

The facility opens in early August for two weeks, giving prospective buyers the chance to examine the horses before a two-day auction held in the Humphrey S. Finney Sales Pavilion. In addition to breeders and buyers, the public is also welcome to observe the proceedings. The horses are paraded around the well-kept lot, in front of their stalls, or around a small oval, where potential buyers carefully scrutinize a number of traits. A worthy steed is characterized by long legs, well-angled shoulders, a lean body with defined musculature, a deep chest, and a spirited and intelligent demeanor. Interested parties look at the horses' teeth, feel their hocks, observe their gait, and examine the hooves for cracks.

The grounds, which were extensively renovated in 2009, are decorated by facility staff with colorful beds of annuals and window boxes. Many of the individual stables provide their own flower baskets, which are hung along the front of the horse stalls. The occasional perennial border on the grounds contains varieties that bloom in late summer, such as black-eyed Susan and coneflower. Even the fence around the perimeter is softened with climbing trumpet vines and clematis.

Considering the brief time the facility is open, the staff and companies who represent the breeders go to great lengths to provide a colorful backdrop of flowers that make the horse-buying experience more pleasant.

Right: In keeping with Saratoga tradition, the stables and offices at the Fasig-Tipton grounds are enlivened with colorful plantings and window boxes. *Opposite:* Statues of the legendary Secretariat grace the courtyard garden and patio at the National Museum of Racing and Hall of Fame.

Preserving History

The National Museum of Racing and Hall of Fame was founded in 1950 by a group led by Cornelius Vanderbilt Whitney. It was originally located in the Canfield Casino before being moved in 1955 to its present location on Union Avenue across from the thoroughbred track. The museum, which chronicles the history of the sport, has been upgraded over the years, housing a superb collection of racing memorabilia, an interactive exhibit, and galleries.

The museum has two gardens, including a small outdoor space on the building's east side. A spacious brick patio, decorated with wooden benches and a classic tiered fountain at the center, is surrounded by lush plantings of summer-blooming shrubs and perennials. Just beyond a waist-high black iron fence, the bricks extend to a life-size bronze statue of Seabiscuit, sculpted by Hughlette "Tex" Wheeler around 1940. The legendary horse was owned by Charles Howard, who commissioned the statue. When Howard's California home was sold, the statue was donated to the museum by his family in the mid-1990s. Hydrangeas, barberries, clipped evergreen shrubs, and ground covers soften the area around the base of the statue.

A small open courtyard garden inside the museum is the site of another bronze statue, one of horse racing's most recent Triple Crown winners, Secretariat. The sculpture, made by John Skeaping, was a gift from Paul Mellon to the museum. A prominent thoroughbred owner and breeder, Mellon is the son of former U.S. Treasury secretary Andrew Mellon.

In 2002, the courtyard garden was renovated by Robin Wolfe, with the backing of the late Georgiana Ducas, a long-time Saratoga gardener and a member of the Pillsbury family. The garden now holds a diverse collection of hydrangeas, burgundy-leaved Japanese maples (*Acer palmatum*), purple ninebark (*Physocarpus opulifolius*), evergreens, and other shrubs. The landscape is meant to be low maintenance and have year-round interest. The box hedges along the inside viewing windows were selected for their tolerance to weather extremes and the weight of winter snows.

A Landscape That's a Sure Bet

Just south of the thoroughbred race course on Nelson Avenue is Saratoga Gaming and Raceway. The original half-mile oval harness track, built in 1941, has seen its own share of illustrious equines, trainers, and owners. The horses, known as standardbreds, are trained to race at a trot or pace rather than at a run, and their drivers are pulled behind them in small carriages known as sulkies.

In 2004, the Racino, as it is known locally, was opened on the track grounds, becoming one of the first gaming facilities in New York State. The combination of video gaming and live simulcasts from other racing venues has revitalized the track, drawing 2.2 million visitors a year and generating millions in revenue. Several restaurants and bars, a food court, a night club, and evening racing make this full-service venue a popular destination after a day at the flat track.

The facility, which is open year-round, takes on the long-standing citywide tradition of flower decorating with gusto. Changing displays of spring bulbs, summer annuals, fall chrysanthemums, and Christmas decorations make the grounds festive in all four seasons. During the growing season, a total of seventy beds are planted, including the street entrances and around the parking areas. There are flower boxes on the grandstand's exterior and plantings in the center of the oval. At the Racino's south entrance, a large circular island and a series of beds along the covered promenade are spectacularly planted with lush, colorful flowers.

The mastermind behind the lavish plantings is Sally Nizolek, the head gardener who has worked at the Racino since 1998. A self-taught gardener with a background in art, Nizolek relies on her artistic training and eye for color to design the beds. Most of the thirty thousand annuals and perennials planted each year are grown from seeds, cuttings, or plugs (small starts) in two large greenhouses on Nelson Avenue. Nonhardy bulbs such as dahlias, canna lilies, and elephant's ears are saved from year to year, dug in fall and overwintered in the greenhouses.

Spring bulbs, primarily daffodils *(Narcissus)* but also tulips, allium, and crocus, offer a welcome respite from the long, cold winter. Deer are a problem, so daffodils, which are distasteful to deer, are the most successful. The major plantings are installed in late spring for peak bloom during the tourist season in July and August. The two-person year-round landscaping staff swells with the addition of three part-timers in summer to assist with the labor-intensive upkeep.

Because the facility is so large, the beds are planted with bold designs to be in scale with the buildings and the surrounding countryside scenery. In a single border, some varieties are planted together in drifts and repeated at intervals along the bed. Other plants are spaced in long rows, tying the colors together. The large swaths of color and repetition are design principles that give definition to the display and keep individual plants from being lost in the shuffle.

Bold color at the Racino: petunias, black-eyed Susan, marigolds, and hibiscus paint a bright tapestry.

Specimens with big leaves and colorful foliage are used for dramatic visual impact. Canna 'Tropicanna', with sensational striped leaves of brilliant orange, red, and purple, contrasts sharply with adjacent chartreuse 'Golden Delicious' pineapple sage *(Salvia elegans* 'Golden Delicious'). A favorite plant is elephant's ear, which was popular during Victorian times. Besides the traditional green-leaved varieties, newer cultivars come in shades of deep purple, dusky burgundy, and yellow-green, with additional characteristics such as ruffling and colored veins and undersides. The ends of some of the beds are planted with large clumps of elephant's ear, providing a focal point that draws the eye into the rest of the landscape.

Nizolek enjoys experimenting with different cultivars. *Alternanthera* 'Royal Tapestry' *(A. dentata* 'Royal Tapestry') has strappy leaves with perpendicular branching and foliage color in copper, burgundy, or purple. The versatile bedding plant is perfect in containers or massed in front of a border, where it complements most other plants around it. Another favorite plant is African rosemallow *(Hibiscus acetosella)*, which has deep purple leaves that resemble those of Japanese maple. Unlike more familiar cultivars of hibiscus, the cultivar is grown primarily for its attractive lacy foliage. Nizolek also likes mixing together the many new varieties of coleus that have come on the market in recent years.

The island bed at the south entrance to the Racino, like most of the other beds, changes yearly. A few plants, such as perennial black-eyed Susan *(Rudbeckia* 'Goldsturm'), pink phlox, and orange daylilies at the center remain from year to year. Annuals with an exceptional spreading habit are preferred, as it helps to keep costs down if fewer plants are needed. Nizolek favors 'Vista' Supertunias, a series of petunias that spread over several feet and need no deadheading. She also plants 'Profusion' zinnias, which come in shades of white, orange, and red. A single plant can reach fifteen inches across. They are also mildew and disease resistant and are more tolerant of weather extremes than other zinnia varieties.

Nizolek has a few tricks to make the plants larger and more lush. The beds are amended with city compost, and a new layer four to six inches thick is applied each spring. Osmocote, a timed-release fertilizer, provides a steady source of nutrients all summer. The plants are watered regularly and thoroughly. Beds are routinely inspected for problems, and plants that are damaged by disease, insects, or deer are replaced as needed.

The millions who visit the Racino each year may not come for the flowers, but the landscape is a marvelous attraction on its own. It's one of Saratoga's best-kept secrets that many nongambling locals don't even know about. As the word spreads, the Racino may become as renowned for its winning floral displays as it is for its gambling.

A long perennial border greets Racino visitors at the Nelson Avenue entrance. *Above left:* Intensely planted beds include red salvia, cannas, zinnias, elephant's ear, and hibiscus.

Paying Homage to Tradition

The Saratoga Race Course takes its many traditions seriously. There are many little things that make this thoroughbred meet a uniquely personal experience. Perhaps it's the dappled shade of the paddock, its fence outlined with rows of bright red salvia, where the horses prance with anticipation as their jockeys are mounted before a big race. It might be the imposing grandstand and clubhouse adorned with red-and-white-striped awnings and long flower boxes filled with trailing ivy and annual geraniums (*Pelargonium*). Maybe it's the roar of the crowd as a blur of brightly colored jockey silks and pounding hooves round the top of the stretch against a backdrop of the pastoral infield. Or perhaps it's the ethereal mist rising over the horses' early-morning workout as observers linger over a trackside breakfast, the spicy scent of geraniums wafting from the grandstand flower boxes. There is something nearly sacred about this place and its long and storied past. The ghosts of bygone legends, both two and four legged, that have roamed these grounds for more than 145 years are almost palpable.

Flowers have been part of these timeless rituals since the 1890s, when the city's love affair with plants began with the popular floral fêtes. Historic photos show the track's earliest plantings. A row of flowering shrubs, most likely hydrangeas, were planted between the outer rail and the spectator area along the clubhouse apron. Long boxes filled with dazzling flower displays stretched across the entire front of the grandstand. A multitiered fountain at the end of the grandstand was surrounded with planted island beds. The paddock was decorated with rectangular beds of annuals surrounded by formal lawns that were intersected by walking paths. A small lake with spouting fountains in the infield was rimmed with neatly clipped hedges and rows of flowers. A circular bed, most likely at one of the main entrances, was planted with tropical elephant's ear and decorated with classic statuary and fountains.

Today, much of the track's ambiance is still owed to the proliferation of flowers planted throughout the sprawling grounds. Colorful blooms are found everywhere: the begonia-filled jockey statue island at the clubhouse entrance, the long rows of ivy-draped flower boxes along the grandstand, the salvia-lined paddock, the groomed infield, and the backstretch barns decorated with hanging baskets. The main spectator entrances contain large drifts of impatiens, and median beds along Union Avenue between Exit 14 and Nelson Avenue are planted with bold drifts of annual spider flower or canna lilies surrounded by bedding plants of ageratum, coleus, dahlias, and begonias. Small shade trees are surrounded by neat mounds of shade-loving impatiens.

The behind-the-scenes planning occurs long before the first "Call to the Post" is played by veteran trumpeter Sam the Bugler. Most of the sixty thousand bedding plants are supplied by Dehn's Flowers, a tradition that spans five decades. The New York Racing Association (NYRA) grows the rest. Some fifty-five hundred begonias are grown on-site in greenhouses near the Oklahoma training track; the same number of begonias is grown at Belmont Park on Long Island and shipped north by truck. (A partial list from a recent growing year reads like the inventory from an overstocked garden center: thirteen

Above: A flower-filled urn sits atop a stepping stone once used by passengers disembarking from horse-drawn carriages. *Above right:* At the Saratoga Race Course, the grandstand is decorated with well-stocked flower boxes. *Right:* Many of the stables, including that of D. Wayne Lukas, are decorated with plantings.

thousand red and white begonias; thirty-five hundred coleus; twenty-seven hundred geraniums; twenty-five hundred petunias; two thousand trailing ivy; and five hundred canna and gladiolus bulbs.) New starts of German ivy are propagated from cuttings in Dehn's greenhouses and grown out to be used the following season, a practice that goes back many years. Thousands of annual seeds are directly sown in wildflower plots. Once the track opens, watering of the plantings in public areas takes place each Tuesday when the track is "dark" (closed), so that patrons don't get wet from overhanging plants.

Some of NYRA's workers affectionately refer to the annual ritual of planting the track as "dressing up the old lady." The process begins just after Memorial Day and continues until the Fourth of July. The racetrack employees are responsible for planting most of the begonias, especially those around the jockey statue island at the clubhouse entrance. The grouping of lawn jockeys in the oval represents twelve of the year's previous stakes winners, with each individual statue painted in the winner's stable colors. Dehn's sends over a crew of three or four of their own staff to plant the flowers supplied by the nursery. One long-time employee, Janice Taylor, has been decorating the track for more than twenty-five years. She knows the place like the back of her hand, and has the planting routine down pat.

The flower boxes that grace the front of the four-story clubhouse are planted with green trailing ivy, petunias, and annual geraniums in the track's colors of red and white. The geraniums are especially selected to grow tall enough to fit the scale of the boxes, so as not to be dwarfed by the ivy. The area in back of the grandstand is shaded by deciduous trees (mostly maples), so the boxes are planted with ivy, impatiens, or shade-tolerant varieties of coleus in bright hues and variegations. Classic white urns containing spiky dracaena and trailing ivy geraniums stand sentinel by the clubhouse exits.

Before each race, the jockeys and horses parade around the paddock so that spectators can evaluate the contenders before placing their bets. Once the jockeys are mounted, they make a final promenade past bright rows of annual red salvia, dusty miller, and blue ageratums. At the center of the paddock is a life-size statue of Sea Hero (winner of the 1993 Kentucky Derby and Travers Stakes), surrounded by yellow plumed cockscomb (*Celosia argentea*). Just beyond the paddock is Big Red Spring, one of Saratoga's famous mineral springs.

Many of the backstretch barns are decorated with flower beds of annuals and hanging baskets. Trainers and stable owners bring in their own plantings. The waste material generated by the horses is recycled for agricultural use. Much of the straw and manure mixture that is mucked out of the horse stalls is trucked to a farm in Pennsylvania, where it is used as a medium for growing mushrooms.

Pieces of the racetrack's history have been integrated into the landscape. Planters in front of the maintenance facilities were made from old megaphones that were once part of the public address system. The megaphones were set on pedestals and painted white, then planted with trailing petunias, geraniums, coleus, and spiky dracaena. A coach stepping-stone dating to 1864 was used to disembark race goers from their horse-drawn carriages. The stone, located in back of the grandstand, is now used as a pedestal for a large urn filled with trailing ivy, petunias, and geraniums.

Because of the track's historical significance, steps are being taken to preserve and restore the grounds. Facilities manager Charlie Wheeler, who has worked here since 2006, is exploring options for preserving the trees found throughout the property. The thousands of elegant shade trees, many of which have been here for more than a century, have been imperiled by soil compaction caused by cars and motorized equipment and pedestrian and horse traffic. "The entire track is designated a historical landmark, and these trees are an integral part of the beauty and ambiance that make this track so special," Wheeler says. "We have an obligation to see to it these living treasures grace the grounds here for many more decades to come." Plans are under way to bring in a forester to conduct a tree inventory, assess the health of individual specimens, and to reclaim the grounds as an urban park.

In May 2007, the Saratoga Springs Preservation Foundation formed the Saratoga Race Course Coalition to inventory and evaluate the existing buildings and grounds, consisting of more than two hundred structures, including the horse barns, maintenance facilities, administrative complex, and grandstand. The coalition will develop a long-range preservation plan for the track, which is included in one of Saratoga Springs' historic districts. ❧

Above: The tradition of filling the paddock area with flowers dates back many decades. COURTESY SARATOGA ROOM, SARATOGA LIBRARY *Right:* The red and white begonias at the clubhouse entrance represent the track's colors. Each year the lawn jockeys are painted in the colors of the previous year's stakes winners. *Below:* A statue of Sea Hero.

The Floral Tradition at Travers Stakes

Summer in Saratoga culminates with the season's biggest attraction, the Travers Stakes. America's oldest for three-year-olds, the Travers Stakes attracts the top horses with a $1 million purse and is often referred to as the fourth jewel of the Triple Crown. The discourse among racing fans as they speculate over which horse will win runs as heated and passionate as the run-up to any Super Bowl or World Series.

Travers Day in the racetrack clubhouse is like a trip into yesteryear. Fancy hats and elegant sundresses are the order of the day for the ladies, while the gentlemen look snappy in crisp shirts and summer suits. Fine cuisine and cocktails are enjoyed from the comfort of the clubhouse dining area or reserved box seats. Spectators who pack the trackside apron, stretches, and paddock areas come more casually attired in shorts and T-shirts and toting lawn chairs and picnic coolers.

In the mid-1990s, florist Susan Lee Laing, noted that the Travers Stakes lacked a flower blanket to bedeck the winning horse, a tradition observed at the Kentucky Derby and other major racing events. Laing, who is the daughter of the late Bob Lee, former New York Racing Association Commissioner, has a long family association with the racetrack. She contacted the racing association and offered to make one herself. The first Travers Stakes blanket, made at Laing's flower shop, was presented to 1994 winner Holy Bull.

After consulting with others who had made flower blankets, Laing created her own design. Her first blanket, a rectangular one, fit poorly over the horse's withers, so after some trial and error she settled on a pattern that better followed a horse's natural contours.

Fifteen hundred carnations of red and white (the track's colors) are used to make the nearly ten-foot-long tapestry. The color pattern typically consists of a white border and a red background, with a white T at each end. Sturdy carnations are the flower of choice because the blanket needs to be assembled a day in advance of the big race.

Completing the huge blanket in such a short time is more than one person can accomplish, so Laing enlists the help of friends and neighbors. The annual ritual has evolved into a "flower blanket party" held at her home. Some participants return each year, and newcomers fill out the volunteer assembly team. Laing has even been known to recruit complete strangers from the track to help.

Jockey Garrett Gomez and Colonel John in the winner's circle at the 139th Travers Stakes in 2008. Their win-by-a-nose triumph over Mambo in Seattle was one of the most exciting finishes in the race's history.

The party begins around four in the afternoon, when Laing lays the cut-out felt pattern on a large piece of plywood placed over the pool table in her game room, where there is plenty of room to maneuver. Buckets of flowers are hauled upstairs from a basement cooler, and sticks of florist's glue are melted in tiny electric cook pots.

Blanket assemblers come and go throughout the evening, applying flowers in between sips of wine and bites of sandwich from an elaborately prepared spread. There are designated tasks, from stem cutting and needle threading to flower sewing. After the stem is removed, each bloom is glued to the felt backing, then hand-sewn with a curved upholstery needle for additional reinforcement. The blanket is usually finished sometime in the late evening or early the next morning, depending on how many people show up to help.

By nine on the morning of the Travers Stakes, the flower tapestry is carefully loaded into a pickup truck and transported to the race course. There it is displayed adjacent to the jockey's room, where riders pause to touch it for luck before the big race.

Laing's duties on Travers Day aren't over once the blanket is delivered. As soon as the winning horse is announced, she heads to her family's Wishing Well Restaurant to paint the lawn jockey out front in the winning stable's colors before patrons arrive to celebrate with a post-victory meal.

For Susan Lee Laing, having a hand in making Saratoga's biggest day happen is its own reward.

The grounds at Yaddo are the back-drop for a rich collection of sculpture. Here, *Morning, Noon, and Night* faces the grand Yaddo mansion. *Opposite:* A nymph from the woodland garden pool fountain.

Yaddo: Artistry
AND Horticulture

*I*n the latter part of the nineteenth century, Saratoga's more prosperous summertime visitors eschewed the grand hotels, taking up residence in "summer cottages" they built around the city. Many were actually grand mansions with elaborate grounds and a full staff. Some illustrious families would remain year-round, becoming distinguished members of the community.

In 1881, Wall Street financier Spencer Trask purchased a four-hundred-acre tract of land just east of the Saratoga Race Course. Trask was an astute businessman, the director of several railroads and president of the Edison Illuminating Company, which brought Thomas Edison's numerous inventions, including the light bulb, to fruition.

The original property, owned by Jacobus Barhyte, a Revolutionary War veteran who fought at the Battles of Saratoga, included a farm, gristmill, tavern, and residence. Spencer and his wife, Katrina, lived in the existing house until it burned down ten years later. In its place, they built an impressive fifty-five-room mansion inspired by Haddon Hall in

England. The granite Queen Anne–style home, designed by New Jersey architect William Halsey Wood, took two years to build and was completed in 1893. The estate was named Yaddo at the suggestion of the Trask's young daughter, Christina.

The family embraced their adopted community, becoming great patrons of the arts, as Katrina was an accomplished playwright, novelist, and poet in her own right. Spencer was instrumental in protecting the region's mineral springs, which had become compromised from overuse.

The setting of Yaddo was almost heavenly, with mature maple and conifer forests draping the gently sloping hills, and ponds plentiful with fish, their banks teeming with wildlife. In 1899, Spencer commissioned a formal European-style rose garden as a birthday gift to his beloved Katrina. Hundreds of roses were planted in four symmetrical quadrants at the base of a small rise, with a pool and fountain as the centerpiece. Three elevated stone terraces overlooked the rose beds. A grand marble staircase rose to

Yaddo in the fall. *Above:* The Queen Anne–style mansion. Koi swim in the rose garden fountain. *Center and right:* A classical portico leads to the rose garden, which is flanked by four statues representing the seasons. Here, the statue *Fall* is complemented by a backdrop of autumn foliage.

a balcony with sweeping views of the Hudson River Valley and beyond to the Green Mountains of Vermont. Behind the balcony, a 180-foot-long pergola, constructed with Roman-style terra-cotta columns, provided a grand and imposing backdrop.

The gardens became an ongoing collaboration between Spencer and Katrina. They wanted to integrate the discipline and order of traditional gardens that they had seen on trips to Europe with a free-flowing style that would reflect their artistic inclinations. The landscape would not be a place to study or label plant varieties but, as Katrina wrote, "a garden of romance—which was not made for the roses, but where the roses bloom for the garden." With Katrina's vision for the garden, combined with her talents as a writer, the garden became known as the Poet's Corner of Yaddo.

Spencer and Katrina thrived in their new community, but despite their great wealth and social status, they were not immune to the realities of the day. Diseases virtually unseen today were rampant, and the mortality rate for the very young was high. Over time, the Trasks would lose all four of their children to illness, two to diphtheria in the same year.

Grief stricken, and without any direct heirs to their estate, Spencer and Katrina were at a loss as to the future of their cherished property. One day, while seeking comfort in the gardens she loved, Katrina experienced an epiphany—"an unseen hand seemed laid upon me," she would later write. She envisioned artists coming to Yaddo, where they would create new work inspired by the bucolic natural setting. She was so taken with the idea that she decided that the estate should be placed in a trust to be used as an artists' retreat.

In 1900, the Trasks formed the Corporation of Pine Garde (later the Corporation of Yaddo), with the purpose of providing a creative environment for artists to have uninterrupted time to think, create, and develop their talents. The trust was administered by George Foster Peabody following the deaths of Spencer in 1909 and Katrina in 1922. A lifelong family friend and Spencer's business partner, Peabody became Katrina's husband in the year before her death.

The retreat, established in 1926, became internationally renowned, hosting nearly six thousand composers, visual artists, and writers as of 2009. Sixty-four Pulitzer Prize winners and hundreds more award-winning artists have honed their craft on the estate's enchanting grounds. Prominent guests have included Leonard Bernstein, Aaron Copland, Sylvia Plath, Mario Puzo, Henri Cartier-Bresson, Philip Roth, Katherine Anne Porter, and Truman Capote. Elisabeth Alexander, a more recent Yaddo alumnus, was chosen to read the inaugural poem at President Barack Obama's swearing-in ceremony in 2009. Famed writer John Cheever said of the estate, "The forty acres on which the principal buildings of Yaddo stand have seen more distinguished activity in the arts than any other piece of ground in the English-speaking community, or perhaps the entire world."

Invited artists are granted two to eight weeks of uninterrupted time to pursue their passion, from music composition to filmmaking. Lodging and meals are provided so residents can focus on their craft. The chance to interact with other artists from all corners of the globe, combined with the tranquil setting, presents a unique opportunity for creativity and a rare break from everyday obligations.

During the latter part of the twentieth century, the treasured gardens tended by Katrina and Spencer fell into disrepair, and some of the statuary was vandalized. In 1991, Saratoga

A Poetic Nod To Time

Just below the pergola, on a balcony overlooking the rose garden, is a sundial (a reproduction of the original). The inscribed verse, which became a classic, was written for Katrina Trask by noted American author and educator Henry van Dyke. It reads:

Time is
Too slow for those who wait
Too swift for those who fear
Too long for those who grieve
Too short for those who rejoice
But for those who Love,
Time is Eternity

On September 6, 1997, some of the Yaddo staff and board members were glued to the television to witness the funeral service at Westminster Abbey for Diana, Princess of Wales. To their great surprise, van Dyke's poem was immortalized to an audience of millions worldwide when it was read by Diana's sister, Lady Jane Fellowes.

Saratoga Springs, N.Y., Rose Garden at Yaddo.

resident Jane Wait founded the Yaddo Garden Association and became its first president. Her late husband, Newman "Pete" Wait, was president of The Adirondack Trust Company, and the family is just one of many benefactors who quietly lend their support to Yaddo and other similar organizations in the Saratoga community.

The association's primary mission was to restore the ten acres of gardens to their former elegance, and to provide the means to maintain them. Volunteers pruned trees and shrubs, pulled weeds, and renewed existing beds with fresh soil and nutrients. Statues and fountains were cleaned and repaired, and the rose beds were replanted with newer, sturdier varieties.

Opposite: The gardens at Yaddo overlooked a spectacular view of the Hudson Valley and Vermont. Today, the view is obscured by trees. Courtesy Saratoga Room, Saratoga Library. *Left:* The natural garden at Yaddo was open and sunny when it was built. Today, it is the site of a shaded native woodland garden. Courtesy of Yaddo, photographer unknown. *Above:* Statues of the four seasons stand along one side of the rose garden.

The Gardens Today

Today, the estate and gardens look much the same as they did when Katrina Trask strolled the grounds a century ago. The Queen Anne mansion still stands atop a gentle crest, overlooking a wide expanse of manicured lawn. At the bottom of the hill, at the edge of a tall stand of white pines, is a fountain with a statue of Dawn as its centerpiece. The massive marble sculpture, dubbed *Morning, Noon, and Night,* was imported from Milan, Italy.

To the south of the fountain is a portico with terra-cotta columns and an iron gate that marks the entrance to the garden. The top of the gate is carved with ST/KT, the Trasks' initials. On either side is a wooded glen planted with native ferns and shade-loving hostas.

In the view beyond the gate, the rose garden unfolds like a grand romantic tapestry. Hundreds of hybrid tea and floribunda roses in red, pink, white, and yellow are laid out in neat rows. Recent introductions include polyanthas and other varieties known for disease resistance and cold hardiness. Enclosing the beds are neatly clipped hedges of barberry, a hardier substitute for the English boxwood typically used to edge formal gardens. A long hedge of rugosa roses on the terraced slope includes varieties used in the original garden. Climbers trained up the columned pergola are a mix of 'William Baffin', 'Blaze', and unidentified old roses in shades of red, white, and pink. Their perfumed scent hangs in the air, permeating the entire garden on a warm summer day.

At the edge of the rose garden stand four marble statues, representing each season. Behind them, in a secluded grove of trees, is the likeness of Christalan, who symbolizes youth, chivalry, and triumph over the earthly bonds of mortality. The sculpture garden was created as a memorial to the Trasks' four children.

The colonnade on the upper terrace separates the rose beds from a more shaded rock garden. Set amongst a hundred-year-old pine grove, the garden offers a cool haven on warm summer days. Katrina designed this section to be informal, a blending of cultivated flowers and the surrounding natural woods. Two pools on different levels are connected with a man-made stream. The centerpiece of the lower pool is a statue of a nymph and a dolphin. In spring, the gardens come alive with ferns, Canadian wild ginger *(Asarum canadense)*, phlox *(P. stolonifera)*, columbine *(Aquilegia canadensis)*, Jack-in-the-pulpit *(Arasaema triphyllum)*, Solomon's seal *(Polygonatum)*, trillium *(T. grandiflorum)*, and cranesbill geranium. The deeply shaded area is lightened up with ground covers with foliage interest, including golden creeping Jenny *(Lysimachia nummularia* 'Aurea'), several kinds of nettle *(Lamium)*, and bishop's hat *(Epimedium)*. Later blooms include astilbe, ligularia, bee balm, hydrangea, hosta, peonies, and iris, many selected for their tolerance for shade and moist soil.

Left to right: A statue of Christalan stands behind the rose garden. Trillium and violets in the woodland garden. A twig-style gate at the edge of the woodland garden.

Crowned with a dramatic pergola, the rose garden was a birthday gift to Katrina Trask from her husband.

Roses for the North Country

Because of the long winters and harsh climate in the North Country, roses are a challenge to grow. The most common problem that gardeners face is choosing the wrong varieties. Hybrid teas and other grafted types tend to be less hardy and often die back to the ground, leaving just the rootstock.

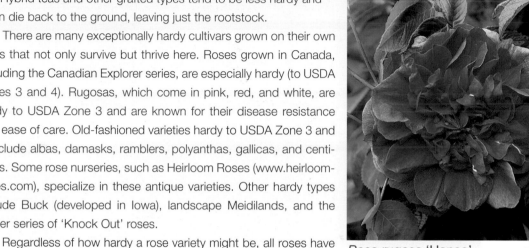

There are many exceptionally hardy cultivars grown on their own roots that not only survive but thrive here. Roses grown in Canada, including the Canadian Explorer series, are especially hardy (to USDA Zones 3 and 4). Rugosas, which come in pink, red, and white, are hardy to USDA Zone 3 and are known for their disease resistance and ease of care. Old-fashioned varieties hardy to USDA Zone 3 and 4 include albas, damasks, ramblers, polyanthas, gallicas, and centifolias. Some rose nurseries, such as Heirloom Roses (www.heirloom-roses.com), specialize in these antique varieties. Other hardy types include Buck (developed in Iowa), landscape Meidilands, and the newer series of 'Knock Out' roses.

Rosa rugosa 'Hansa'

Regardless of how hardy a rose variety might be, all roses have the same basic requirements: lots of sun, good drainage, adequate water, and rich soil amendments of compost or manure. Pruning back dead canes and old shoots in spring can help air circulation and reduce disease. Some newer varieties are specifically bred for low maintenance and disease resistance, making them easier to care for.

Since the rose garden was planted a century ago, the surrounding pine trees have grown, casting more shade and obscuring the valley view. Because roses do best in full sun, the limited light has proved a challenge in preserving the original integrity of the gardens. Newer varieties have been substituted for their tolerance to shade, winter cold, and disease.

The grand pergola, made of plaster, was the main feature of the rose garden. Over time, the terra-cotta structure began crumbling from the harsh exposure to North Country winters. The Yaddo Garden Association initiated an ambitious fund-raising effort, raising the $400,000 needed to restore the pergola. It was reconstructed by Boston Valley Terra Cotta, near Buffalo, New York, one of only two businesses in the United States equipped to perform this specialized process. Western Building Restoration, based in Albany, completed the installation in 2008. Volunteers with the Yaddo Garden Association continue to maintain the gardens, cleaning up the beds in early spring and keeping the roses pruned, fertilized, and watered during the growing season. Though the mansion is closed to the public to ensure the privacy of the resident artists, the gardens and adjacent grounds are open to the public free of charge from dawn to dusk. The serenity and beauty of this lasting gift from the Trasks is a much-treasured part of the community, offering respite to locals, tourists, and the artists who live and work here. ❧

GREENHOUSE. — MRS. J. BLAIR SCRIBNER
SARATOGA SPRINGS. N.-Y.

Skidmore: A Gardener's Legacy

The mineral springs of Saratoga have influenced the city's destiny in often-unexpected ways, attracting people who would prove to have a significant and lasting impact. One of these luminaries was Lucy Skidmore Scribner, the young widow of J. Blair Scribner (son of book publisher Charles Scribner). Her own health failing, Lucy came to Saratoga after her husband's untimely death to seek refuge in the healing powers of the spring waters.

In 1897, Scribner purchased a home and several lots on the west side of North Broadway. An avid gardener, she later acquired another dozen parcels on the opposite side of the elm-lined boulevard, where she created a parklike setting of flower beds and meandering footpaths among the towering pines. A large glass

Left: Lucy Skidmore Scribner's former residence is now home to the Skidmore College president. *Top:* Scribner purchased additional lots across from her home and developed extensive gardens along tree-lined pathways. Courtesy Saratoga Room, Saratoga Library
Right: Her flower-bedecked carriage, ready for one of Saratoga's Floral Fêtes. Page 85
PHOTOS COURTESY SKIDMORE COLLEGE SPECIAL COLLECTIONS

greenhouse and gardener's cottage were located on the expansive parcel, which overlooked the Green Mountains of Vermont.

Scribner also tended gardens in the yard surrounding her home. The front was landscaped with flowering hydrangeas, roses, ornamental grasses, and mature shade trees; there were also many potted plants. In the backyard was a formal European-style garden with geometric beds of trees and flowers with statuary at the center. Potted dracaenas, Norfolk Island pines, and ferns adorned a glassed-in porch, where Scribner enjoyed sitting.

Recognizing the need for greater educational opportunities for women, Scribner opened the Young Women's Industrial Club of Saratoga in 1903. She purchased the buildings and grounds of the former Temple Grove Seminary to house her fledgling school. The academy, with a curriculum emphasizing the arts, quickly expanded and was chartered in 1911 as the Skidmore School of Arts. Eleven years later, it would become the certified four-year liberal arts school known as Skidmore College.

The original campus, located east of Congress Park, expanded along with its burgeoning attendance. Former homes and commercial buildings in a several block radius were acquired on Union Avenue, Circular Street, Spring Street, and other streets. The Skidmore campus eventually grew to comprise more than eighty buildings on forty acres.

Scribner, who passed away in 1931, willed the bulk of her estate to the college she founded. Her home was eventually occupied by several private owners until the property was reacquired by the school in 1964. Today, Scribner's former home is still beautifully landscaped and is now the residence of Skidmore's president. The former gardener's cottage is now a private residence.

During the early 1960s, the administration began looking at options to relocate the college in order to consolidate and expand its operations. J. Erik Jonsson, a board trustee and the president of Texas Instruments, provided the funds to purchase a thousand-acre tract for a new campus that was part of the former Woodlawn estate. The parcel, adjacent to North Broadway, was once owned by Judge Henry Walton, one of the area's earliest landholders. Walton had sold a 130-acre parcel to Gideon Putnam in 1805 that would become the original village of Saratoga. The scenic Woodlawn property was later acquired by Judge Henry Hilton, who developed the 1,300-acre estate into one of the largest privately owned parks in the country. In an ironic twist, Lucy Skidmore Scribner wanted to buy the property for the school fifty years earlier but was unsuccessful.

Construction of the new Skidmore campus began in 1963 and was completed in 1971, the same year the school became coeducational. Other buildings have since been added. Today, the private liberal arts institution, with an enrollment of 2,400 students, is nationally recognized for its dance, music, theater, and visual arts programs. The complex

of modern-style buildings was brilliantly integrated with its natural wooded setting. Many of the original mature shade trees were preserved in spacious courtyards with walkways that connect the dormitories and academic structures. Floor-to-ceiling bay windows blur the distinction between the indoors and the bucolic scenery. A large wooded area of hardwood maples adjacent to the campus, a favorite place for hiking and exploring, is known as the North Woods. The walking trails are remnants of the bridle and carriage paths of the former Woodlawn estate.

An Old Campus Gets New Life

Some of the former Skidmore buildings were converted into a group of multiple-unit dwellings, aptly named the Skidmore Apartments. The richly landscaped grounds of the sixteen-building complex are overseen by Edward Foley, who has been a groundskeeper here since 1985. Foley is responsible for maintaining the trees, shrubs, and lawns at the complex, which borders Congress Park and stretches along Circular, Spring, Regent, and Court Streets. He began planting flowers here and there, adding more beds until most of the buildings had their own gardens.

Top left: Greenhouses and winding paths in Lucy Skidmore's garden. COURTESY SKIDMORE COLLEGE SPECIAL COLLECTIONS. *Left and top right:* The former Skidmore Hall is now home to an apartment complex.

Autumn foliage at the former Surrey WIlliamson estate.
Opposite: the memorial gardens contain artwork make by alumni.

Foley is a self-taught gardener, absorbing ideas from books and magazines and experimenting with different plants to find the right combinations. The focus is to maximize color rather than striving for a formal design. He favors brightly hued flowers that bloom over a long time, and reliable foliage bedding plants such as coleus. Foley's interest in flowers was sparked as a child, when he helped his father weed and water the plants at a well-known local estate. His mother was also an avid gardener.

The urban gardens were started by Foley to dress up the apartment buildings, which he felt looked somewhat institutional. For some of the structures, such as the old Skidmore Hall or the classic brick facades of the Knickerbocker House (once the language center) and the Strong House (the former residence of the college president), the plantings only enhanced their timeless beauty.

Foley prepares the flower beds in spring, adding peat moss, compost, and manure to create a healthy foundation. With a planting budget from the management, he purchases flats of red and blue salvia, old-fashioned orange and yellow marigolds with golf ball–size blooms, sweetly scented alyssum, blue ageratum, dusty miller, and petunias for the sunny areas. Impatiens, begonia, and coleus brighten up more shaded spots. Perennials such as Shasta daisy (*Leucanthemum* x *superbum*), black-eyed Susan, and hosta are gradually being integrated to reduce the amount of maintenance. Foley seeks advice from the Cornell Cooperative Extension when challenged with a unique insect, disease, or cultivation issue.

Tenants and passersby have taken notice of Foley's plantings. In 2007, the Skidmore Apartments were recognized in a citywide floral contest as one of the best commercial spaces. While he is tending the beds, Foley is often stopped by neighbors and visitors, who ask questions or compliment him on the landscape. Many older tenants of the apartments sit outside their buildings on benches or chairs where they can take in the colorful view. Seeing the enjoyment that others get from his horticultural creations is reward enough for Foley. "With all of the bad things happening in the world today, it's important to stop and smell the flowers," he says.

Surrey Williamson

Soon after the Skidmore campus was moved to its current location, the college purchased several properties on North Broadway. One of these was the ten-acre estate of E. Clarence Jones, a New York City stockbroker. The English Tudor–style home, built in 1918, was a replica of a manor that Jones had admired in England's Cotswold district. The estate, which Jones named Broadview Lodge, included the twenty-one-room main house, the superintendent's quarters, various farm buildings, and a garage. The wooded grounds were beautifully landscaped with stone walls, flower beds, a goldfish pool, statuary, and a sunken garden in an area named the East View. An impressive stone pergola led from the garden to a tennis court.

Jones died in 1926, and the property was eventually sold to Mrs. Amscott Wilson, a wealthy horse owner who used the estate as her summer home. It was resold in 1945 and converted into the Brown School for Boys, a private boarding academy. The property changed hands again before being acquired by Skidmore College in 1967 through a gift-

purchase arrangement. The upper floor of the main house, now the Surrey Williamson Inn, has overnight accommodations for college trustees, alumni, and other guests. Private receptions, meetings, and other school functions are held in the elegantly decorated ground-level rooms. The former superintendent's cottage is now the Colton Alumni Welcome Center. A garage-annex that also included a chauffeur's apartment was expanded and is now the Eissner Admissions Center.

The expansive property is beautifully landscaped with evergreens, including stately blue spruce, and a wide variety of older shade trees with brilliant fall color. Around the main house, trees and shrubs in varying heights and hues create a richly layered tapestry. A grand stone staircase leads from the south porch down to a grass terrace enclosed by a stone wall and railing; a stucco antique sundial on a stone pedestal serves as the centerpiece. The spacious lawn gently slopes down to the sunken garden.

In 2002, several Skidmore alumni decided to renovate the East View garden to hold a ceremony there for deceased classmates as part of their forty-fifth reunion. Florence Andresen, Barbara Mansfield Saul, Elizabeth Hartz Hewitt, and Marge O'Meara Storrs, all in the class of 1957, worked on the neglected space. They cleared, pruned, and weeded the circular garden and planted 650 impatiens in shades of pink and white. Their efforts were well received, and it was decided to turn the garden into a permanent memorial for all Skidmore graduates.

The original space included formal rose beds designed in four quadrants around a circular fishpond. Pathways radiated out from the pool in a spokelike formation to the sunken stone walls. As part of the renovation, the granite walls were repaired and reinforced. The stone-columned pergola, once covered with lattice and vining wisteria, has gently settled into the landscape. Local slate, formerly part of the fish pond, was replaced with gray cobblestones. The pagoda-style roof of a stone alcove with built-in wooden seats was refurbished.

Each of the quadrants was rebuilt to represent four decades of Skidmore classes (past and future), with every class since 1903 having its own engraved brick. The area between the beds and the grass pathways is edged with stone, and the wedge-shaped sectors are landscaped with creeping myrtle *(Vinca minor)* anchored with Japanese flowering dogwoods *(Cornus kousa)*. The trees, which are kept pruned to retain their umbrella shape, come alive with drifts of white flowers in late spring, producing strawberry-like red berries later in the season.

Benches, planters, and statuary were created by some of the many talented artists who have passed through the halls of Skidmore College. Ceramist Jill Fishon-Kovachik (class of 1981) made the stone urns that grace the perimeter of the stone terrace. Faculty

Clockwise from left: Gardens at the Colton Alumni Center. The Memorial garden. Stone steps lead to the walled garden.

The walled gardent and *(right)* the pergola at the Surrey Williamson estate.

artist Leslie Ferst (class of 1976) embellished the outside of the planters with a cycle-of-life motif. The urns are planted with spiky dracaena and colorful specimens of coleus. Custom teakwood memorial benches were built by John Danzer (class of 1975), owner of the New York City–based exterior design firm Munder-Skiles (www.munder-skiles.com).

The centerpiece of the Alumni Memorial Garden was created by Vermont artist Barbara Stroock Kaufman (class of 1940). The stone sculpture is the likeness of Bhumi Devi, the Hindi goddess of the cycle of life. Kaufman's penchant for Asian style was influenced by time she spent living in Cambodia.

The garden is supported by donations from trustees and former students, who have the option of giving live plants as a remembrance. One patron left an endowment that provides for new plants each year. The garden is maintained by a staff of dedicated volunteers, along with support from campus staff. A general cleanup is done in spring, and the gardeners return each month during the summer to weed, prune, and maintain the pots. An irrigation system on automatic timers keeps things watered.

The space is used each year during reunion weekend, but it has also become known as a place for quiet respite and reflection. More than just a tribute to the school's past students, the garden is a peaceful sanctuary that is enjoyed throughout the growing season by students and locals alike. ⚜

THE *Grand Mansions*

By the 1870s, Saratoga had become one of America's most popular resorts, attracting tourists ranging from some of the nation's most illustrious families to those of more modest means. Accommodations included the grand hotels with all the latest amenities, more moderate hostelries, and small boarding houses. As the wealthy and elite spent more time in Saratoga, however, they chose to build their own summer "cottages" rather than stay in the hotel resorts. Actually grand, elaborate homes designed by renowned architects of the time, the cottages were concentrated on Circular Street, Upper Broadway, and Union Avenue. Other fine homes in a wide array of architectural styles were sprinkled along Spring Street, Phila Street, Madison Street, Fifth Avenue, and other east-side streets.

Saratoga's decline as a premier resort destination following World War II also marked the decline of Saratoga's "Great Ladies," as the mansions are sometimes referred to. Some, such as the incomparable Mabee house, were razed by fire; others fell into disrepair and were torn down. Fortunately, many were preserved and restored during Saratoga's revival beginning in the 1970s, and today these historic landmarks are a large part of Saratoga's elegant and timeless atmosphere.

At twenty thousand square feet, the Riggi mansion on North Broadway is one of the largest private residences in Saratoga. *Opposite:* Detail from a fountain at the Batcheller Mansion Inn

Formal English Style on Broadway

The Brackett House, located on picturesque, tree-lined North Broadway, was built by Edgar T. Brackett and his wife, Emma, in 1885. Designed by noted architect S. Gifford Slocum, the brick and wood facade was created in the late Victorian–Queen Anne style.

Educated as a lawyer, Brackett was elected to the New York State Senate, representing the district that included Saratoga. He was the founder and first president of The Adirondack Trust Company, a venerable local banking institution that still serves the community. Brackett was also a prominent community leader who was instrumental in getting the 1908 Anti-Pumping Act passed, saving the area's mineral springs from certain devastation. The iron gates at the main entrance to Congress Park commemorate his early conservation efforts.

The Bracketts resided in their home until 1935, when it was sold and converted into Beverly Manor, a boarding house. It remained so until the 1970s, when it reverted back to a private residence. In 1984, the late Harry V. Quadracci, founder of Quad/Graphics, purchased the home and restored the elegant mansion to its original splendor. Quad/Graphics, which has a branch in Saratoga, is the third-largest printer in the United States, producing magazines including *Time, Newsweek, Sports Illustrated,* and *People.*

The mansion is part of a complex to accommodate out-of-town clients and corporate executives from other branches of Quad/Graphics who are visiting on company business. A former carriage house behind the mansion was renovated into guest quarters and beautifully decorated with Victorian-style furnishings. Part of a second expansion in 1998 included the construction of an English-style walled garden, which is used for entertaining and as a place for guests to relax. The garden was designed by Frank Oatman and Jon Wood (both now retired) of Stone's Throw Gardens in Craftsbury, Vermont, based on Quadracci's great appreciation of European gardens from his world travels.

An eight-foot-high brick wall enclosing the space adjacent to the carriage house was already built when Frank and Jon drew up a plan. They worked in close collaboration with Quadracci, who has created distinctive landscapes at many of his business and personal properties. A garden was designed that included an expansive flagstone patio, elegant fountains and statuary, an imposing pergola, and formal plantings. A glass atrium attached to the carriage house, filled with tropical plants, became an inviting place for guests to sit, especially in winter.

The centerpiece of the walled garden is a large fountain at the edge of the patio, with three statues set amidst finely spraying jets of water. A figurine in the likeness of the harvest goddess Demeter is a J. W. Fiske antique original purchased at the first New York Garden Antiques Show. J. W. Fiske & Company of New York City was the most prominent American manufacturer of iron and zinc garden fountains, urns, and statuary of the nineteenth century. French zinc dolphin statues on either side of the harvest goddess, also found at the show, were created around 1800. Large specimens of maiden grass *(Miscanthus)* were planted on either side of the fountain. Along the adjacent brick walls are pear trees in espalier form (a French method of training plants along a wall or trellis, particularly useful in small spaces). The trees produce delectable fruit in late summer.

Above and far right: The main fountain at the Brackett House contains an original J. W. Fiske statue of the goddess of harvest. *Top left:* Filled with tropical plants, the glass atrium is a welcome place to visit in winter. *Right:* A French blue entry gate provides a handsome contrast to the colors of brick and surrounding foliage.

Benches underneath a nearby arbor covered with Chinese wisteria *(W. sinensis)* offer a cool place to sit in summer. Just beyond the arbor is a formal mixed border masterfully planted in layered heights. Low-growing hostas and ground covers in front graduate to medium-size coneflower, black-eyed Susan, and balloon flower *(Platycodon)* against a backdrop of hardy hibiscus and other shrubs. The perennial beds continue along the brick wall on two sides. The centerpiece of the north border is an eighteenth-century original English stone statue of Dionysus (the god of wine, agriculture, and fertility), with Pan (the Greek god of shepherds and flocks) at the base. At the juncture of the perpendicular borders is a secret alcove with a stone bench, an inviting place to enjoy the gardens or read. The strategic placement of fountains throughout the gardens offers the soothing sound of trickling water, muting the city noises from the nearby street.

The grounds of the original Brackett house are also landscaped with beautiful gardens. A brick driveway leads visitors to a round, stone-rimmed brick fountain at the center of the courtyard. Small copper spigots on the side of the fountain are adorned with tiny horse figurines. A formal brick pathway at the edge of the driveway leads to

a peaceful shade garden, and teak benches flank a round pool with another fountain. The garden includes a variety of spring-blooming plants that fade to subtle shades of cooling green in summer.

At the front of the house, a wrought-iron fence allows a glimpse of the entry garden from the street. Formal brick pathways edged with neatly clipped boxwood wind around a circular garden with a fountain at the center. Inside four boxwood quadrants are red and green angel wings *(Caladium)*; the deeply shaded garden is brightened with impatiens in shades of red, pink, and white. The porch is beautifully decorated with flower boxes and hanging baskets filled with red wax begonias, Million Bells, annual geraniums, and trailing creeping Jenny.

Left: A wisteria-covered pergola divides the main garden of the Brackett House from a sunny perennial border. *Above:* A formal perennial border forms the backdrop for a wishing-well fountain.

Between the main house and the guesthouse is a wood-land strolling garden, with peak bloom early in the season. The shaded space is highlighted by a rich diversity of spring-blooming plants, including azalea, sweet woodruff (*Galium odoratum*), astilbe, candelabra primrose (*Primula*), lungwort (*Pulmonaria*), and Jack-in-the-pulpit. Japanese painted fern (*Athyrium nipponicum* 'Pictum'), maidenhair fern (*Adiantum pedatum*), Canadian wild ginger, and hostas offer foliage interest. Paper birch (*Betula papyrifera*), weeping crabapple (*Malus pendula*), and ginkgo provide a structural canopy and focal points.

The gardens were recognized by the Saratoga Springs Preservation Foundation with an award for Outstanding Achievement in Contextual New Design. For guests who stay at the complex, the gardens offer a lovely respite from the company business that draws them here.

Above and right: Floral displays at the Brackett House entry garden change with the season. *Center:* The brass fixtures on a courtyard fountain are a nod to late owner Harry V. Quadracci's love of horse racing.

Rooted in the Community

Many of Saratoga's most illustrious citizens and the businesses they established have helped shape the community into what it is today. The Adirondack Trust Company, founded by Edgar T. Brackett in 1902, is one of the city's most stalwart institutions. The bank has made it possible for local citizens to buy homes, start businesses, and have a safe place to put their savings. The beautiful Vermont marble facade of the home office, located in the heart of downtown on the corner of Broadway and Lake Avenue, is a well-known landmark. More than a hundred years after its founding, the bank takes pride on conducting business the old-fashioned way, by cultivating long-standing relationships with its customers, a rarity in today's world.

Much of these hometown values can be attributed to the Wait family, which has been associated with the bank for four generations. Newman E. Wait, who became president of the bank in 1937, was succeeded by his son, the late Newman E. "Pete" Wait, Jr., and then his grandson Charles V. Wait, who became the bank's president in 1984. Charles's son Charles V. Wait, Jr. is a vice president. The family is one of many who have given back to the community in many inestimable ways, including its longtime support of Yaddo. Jane Wait, Pete's wife, was the founder of the Yaddo Garden Association, which began restoring the garden back to its original grandeur in the early 1990s. Charles Wait has served on the board of directors, and his wife, Candace, now the program director, has worked at Yaddo in various capacities since 1981.

The Waits' elegant estate on North Broadway has been occupied at various times by three generations of the family, as well as a previous bank president outside the family. The home was built by Sidney Root in 1872 in the Second Empire style. Root died in 1879 and his widow, Maria A. Root, operated the home as the Wayland Mansion, an exclusive boarding house.

Top left: The spacious side porch of the Wait house is screened with potted evergreens and tropicals. *Center:* Fall color enriches the backdrop behind the broad lawn. *Left and right:* Red impatiens are used generously for accent color.

The property changed hands before being purchased in 1918 by Charles Van Deusen, who extensively renovated the house, altering the style to its present Greek Revival facade. A grand two-story outdoor veranda added to the side of the home looks out onto the expansive lawn. Van Deusen, who was president of The Adirondack Trust Company during the 1920s and 1930s, successfully steered the institution through the lean years of the Great Depression. Van Deusen left the house to his banking associate, Newman Wait, Sr. The house was later sold to Willard Grande, who lived here from the 1950s to the 1970s. Newman "Pete" Wait owned the house for a time before his son Charles began occupying it in the 1980s.

Charles and his wife, Candace, have beautifully landscaped the grand first-story porch and yard. The upper-level porch, enclosed with a black wrought-iron railing, is a comfortable outdoor living room complete with a couch, wicker chairs with overstuffed cushions, and free-standing lamps. A grand staircase on the lower level opens onto a wide expanse of lush green lawn. The porch is adorned with large clay pots of conifers, potted tropical palms, and black iron urns planted with scarlet impatiens. In spring, rows of bright red tulips adorn the edges of the front sidewalk. The bulbs are replaced with drifts of large-flowered New Guinea impatiens planted alongside the house, driveway, and front walk and around an antique hitching post. At the back of the property is an alcove with a classic statue, whose origin is unknown.

The Waits' enthusiasm extends to the bank landscaping as well. Charles's father, Pete, who was fascinated with the concept of time, decided to spruce up the bank's parking lot with a sophisticated variation of a sundial called an armillary sphere. He ordered a custom-made sculpture from a company in Connecticut and had it shipped to Saratoga in 1978. The inscription is dedicated to Dr. Charles F. Dowd, who operated the Temple Grove Seminary in the 1800s. Dowd is credited with originat-

ing the system of standard time. He established four U.S. standard time zones for the railroad system, which was the precursor to the worldwide system of twenty-four time zones instituted the following year.

A Beloved City Landmark Preserved

One of Saratoga's most visible and spectacular landmarks is the Batcheller Mansion, located at the intersection of Circular Street and Whitney Place. The ornate home, with its commanding view of Congress Park, was built in 1873 by George Sherman Batcheller, a lawyer and New York State assemblyman. The noted community leader was related to Roger Sherman, a signer of the Declaration of Independence, as well as Daniel Webster, the great American statesman and orator. Batcheller was later appointed a special representative to Egypt by President Ulysses S. Grant. During his illustrious career, Batcheller would accept various other business and diplomatic positions in Europe and Washington, D.C.

The mansion, a High Victorian–Gothic amalgamate, was designed by the Albany firm of Nichols & Halcott in a one-of-a-kind pastiche of French Renaissance, Italianate, and Egyptian styles. Fine architectural detail and ornate decoration, and a domed tower reminiscent of a Russian-style minaret, are just some of the structure's hallmarks. The plans for the building were so unique that it became the first private home in the United States to be patented. Batcheller gave it the Arabic name Kaser-el-Nouzha, meaning "Palace of Pleasure."

Following Batcheller's death in 1908, the house went through several different owners and was nearly demolished in 1973. Yet it managed to survive years of neglect and exposure to the elements and was eventually restored to its former grandeur. The interior is resplendent with elaborate Victorian furnishings and sophisticated touches. Today, the elegant mansion, owned by local developer Bruce J. Levinsky, is operated as an upscale bed-and-breakfast inn (for information, visit www.batchellermansioninn.com).

The grounds were also upgraded, with new shrubs and ornamental plantings in an eclectic blend of formal and cottage styles. Levinsky prefers bold floral displays with lots of color, so annual flowers are generously utilized for summerlong bloom. A brightly hued border along the east porch contains perennial hostas and geraniums mixed with an old-fashioned assortment of annual portulaca, California poppies, sweet william *(Dianthus barbatas)*, snapdragons, cornflowers *(Centaurea cyanus)*, pansies, marigolds, and calendula. Island beds along the sidewalk median are planted with Levinsky's favorite canna lilies and annual geraniums, marigolds, and lobelia. Curbside cement planters spill forth with pale yellow marigolds, blood-red amaranthus, Million Bells, pale pink petunias, and trailing silver Dichondra. Ivy geranium baskets and large potted umbrella trees *(Schefflera)* adorn the quiet veranda.

The elaborate front porch with its unique double staircase is decorated with classical-style urns and potted topiaries. A tiny stone-edged bed between the twin staircases is planted with hostas, giant zinnias, annual geraniums, and Johnny-jump-ups *(Viola)*.

Enclosing a small courtyard garden is a neatly trimmed cedar hedge, providing a soft green backdrop to a formal European-style border that complements the home's

Above: The Batcheller Mansion's formal front garden and side garden in summer.
Opposite: Bold red tulips bring early color to the front garden and elaborate entry staircase.

architecture. A classic fountain at the center of the courtyard is edged by a crescent-shaped perennial border filled with reliable North Country staples: long-blooming geraniums, iris, daylilies, lamb's-ears, coral bells *(Heuchera)*, catmint *(Nepeta)*, Shasta daisies, yarrow *(Achillea)*, lilies, tickseed, astilbe, Russian sage, and roses.

Keyna Karp, who has tended the garden for several years, changes the annual display yearly. She evaluates the soil in early spring, adding fresh topsoil mix as needed. Squirrels are a recurrent problem, so mothballs are placed in the flower beds to deter the persistent creatures. Many of the plants, including the hanging baskets, are grown to order at Phillips Garden View, a small seasonal family-run nursery in nearby Grangerville. Karp enjoys the creative freedom that Levinsky allows her, and cherishes her role in dressing up one of Saratoga's most recognizable landmarks. The guests who stay at the elegant mansion, as well as local citizens, are the true beneficiaries of this rescued treasure, an irreplaceable part of Saratoga's storied history.

Charm on Union Avenue

One of Saratoga's major streets, Union Avenue, was originally constructed as a direct route from Congress Spring to Saratoga Lake. The road, which starts near the heart of the city at the intersection of Circular Street, runs along the Saratoga Race Course and continues past the Northway to the lake. Some of the city's most elegant mansions are on the stretch between Nelson Avenue and Circular Street.

One of these mansions, the Furness House, is a fine example of Queen Anne style. Designed by R. Newton Brezee, one of Saratoga's leading architects, the home was built for George Crippen in 1901 and was later owned by Charles Furness, owner of the daily newspaper the *Glens Falls Times*. The narrow Roman brick used on the lower story and the tower was characteristic of late Victorian–style architecture.

The home was sold to Skidmore College and operated as a freshman dormitory for thirty-four years until the campus was moved to its present location in the 1970s. The structure was then used as a group home before being sold and renovated in 1992. Thomas Fox purchased the house in 2003, and it is now operated as the Union Gables Bed and Breakfast (for information, visit www.uniongables.com).

In 2006, innkeeper Thomas Van Gelder created a formal rose garden in front of the carriage house, which was converted into guest quarters. The rose border is situated along a brick pathway and a patio, where guests can relax. In the center of the patio is a large classic-style fountain and pool surrounded by neatly clipped topiary hedges typically found in European landscapes.

Around the roses, Van Gelder planted divisions of iris and peonies dug from a nearby border, and he added daylilies, daisies, iris, gayfeather (*Liatris*), blanket flower (*Gaillardia* x *grandiflora*), obedient plant, and other sturdy perennials. Sun-tolerant New Guinea impatiens and angel wings, its leaves patterned with red, pink, and green, were placed along the front of the fountain. Other annuals are planted here and there for splashes of color all summer long. Large cast-iron Victorian urns were placed on either side of the fountain and planted with spiky dracaena, petunias, and annual salvia. The gardens continue along the carriage house and extend to the back and along the parking area.

Across a wide expanse of lush green lawn at the eastern edge of the property, repeat plantings of clipped hedges and roses are punctuated by ornate black iron benches set against a backdrop of lattice fencing. A spacious brick patio along the side of the house, with the scenic backdrop of lawn and gardens, is the perfect setting for the many weddings, parties, and charity luncheons held throughout the summer season. Plans are under way to construct a formal Colonial-style garden on the home's west side.

The garden is occasionally a source of unexpected surprises. One fall, when Van Gelder was preparing dinner, he threw some squash seeds out the kitchen door into the flower bed. The next spring, the seeds sprouted, and by late summer the vines had clamored

Set in beautifully landscaped grounds, the Furness House, built in 1901, is one of Saratoga's most elegant Victorian mansions. It is now the Union Gables Bed and Breakfast.

ten feet or more among the flowers. Volunteer seedlings of angel's trumpets (*Datura*) and tomatoes are allowed to self-sow and claim the spot where they sprout. One year, a small patch of multicolored decorative Indian corn became an impromptu food source for the neighborhood squirrels. Van Gelder feels that a little surprise here and there makes for a more interesting landscape.

In scale with the home's grand facade, generous drifts of long-blooming perennials flank the front sidewalk. Among them are Russian sage, hosta, coneflower, phlox, mophead hydrangeas, and cotoneaster. The area around the spacious front veranda is softened with hardy shrubs, including barberry (*Berberis*), yew, spirea, and cinquefoil (*Potentilla*). Colorful annual baskets are hung across the porch, and large ferns and palms set among the casual wicker furniture lend a distinctly Victorian feel. For guests who attend special events or stay overnight, the Victorian-style gardens are a classic landscape in a timeless setting.

Left: A classic fountain is the garden centerpiece at Union Gables. *Above:* The renovated carriage house provides additional guest quarters.

An Elegant Landscape

The Hall residence, one of North Broadway's most elegant homes, was built c. 1900 for Troy shirt manufacturer William Lord Hall. The twenty-room mansion on two acres is a fine representation of the Colonial Revival style. Historic postcards show that elegant formal gardens were part of the landscape since the home's inception. Hall occupied the home until the 1920s; then it changed hands over the next several decades.

In 1965, the home was given to Skidmore College by racing fan and horse owner Charles Wilson, who used it only during the race season. Until 1986, it was used as a residence for the college president Joseph C. Palomountain. His wife, Anne, renovated the house and gardens, bringing in trees, shrubs, lilacs, and wisteria from a nursery in Connecticut. Most of the new plants, which included maple and cherry trees, were donated. A new irrigation system was made possible through the generosity of a college trustee, while cuttings of the groundcover Japanese spurge *(Pachysandra terminalis)* were donated by another college trustee's wife, who helped plant them. The spacious yard with its formal gardens was often used for school functions, including commencement events.

In 1986 the home was bought by Joseph O'Hara, who did major renovations to the estate. The home was again sold, and the current homeowner has a European-style garden that retains the character of the early landscape. A large pergola with a central cupola, which appears in old historic photos, is thought to be original to the yard. A brick path, with a children's playhouse at one end, intersects the long, narrow space into four rectangular quadrants. Strips of lawn separate the path from low, formally clipped hedges that frame the perennial borders on either side. The breezy, cottage-style beds are filled with coneflower, daisies, large-flowered hibiscus, and black-eyed Susan. The owner, who does much of the gardening work by herself, prefers reliable spring-blooming peonies and Oriental poppies. Backing the western border are evergreen hedges and a screen of Boston ivy (*Parthenocissus tricuspidata*). A classic statue at the end of the wisteria-covered pergola lends an Old World flavor.

A large carriage house in back was recently restored, and other renovations have been made to the home. The front walkway is flanked with colorful annuals and formal urns planted with potato vines and petunias. The classic home is an integral part of Saratoga's long and storied affiliation with the well heeled who made the town their summer home.

Glitz and Glamour in the Twenty-first Century

The newest addition to the opulent row of mansions along North Broadway is one of the city's most spectacular estates. Owned by Ron and Michele Riggi, the 20,000-square-foot home, a combination of French Château and Italian Renaissance styles, brings a modern twist to the old-fashioned grandeur of the neighboring nineteenth-century manors. The castle-like bluestone structure, inspired by the couple's worldly travels, took five years to build and was completed in 2003. The stone construction, each piece hand cut and fit together much like a puzzle, is rarely found in modern buildings due to the labor and expense involved.

While the Riggis focused on building their elaborate dream home, they lavished equal attention to the grounds. They felt it was important to treat the property as an extension of their living space, reflecting the care and attention to detail afforded in the home's interior and exterior. They enlisted the help of Rich Morris, owner of Toadflax Nursery in South Glens Falls, to design the walkways, stone walls, and fence, the front entry, and the Italianate pools and cabana in back, in a style to match the house.

To capture some of the feel of the old estate gardens, many of which were lost, Morris studied old photos and street maps from the 1800s to see what North Broadway looked like during the grand Victorian era. Because much of the Riggi landscaping is visible from the street, the construction had to conform to certain city building codes. A low stone wall topped by a black iron fence encloses the gardens from the sidewalk yet allows passersby to look inside the grounds.

Formal gardens with brick walks, statuary, fountains, and a lovely antique pergola complement the elegant style of the Hall residence on North Broadway.

At just under an acre, the property, even though it is an oversize city lot, feels much larger. Various garden rooms are seamlessly woven together by the walkways that connect them. The paths were constructed with Turkish travertine stone, the same material used to build the Coliseum in Rome. The walls were made from Adirondack granite mined from the Comstock quarry near Whitehall. Slate was procured from quarries around Granville, on the Vermont border. The double stone staircase at the main entrance was designed to echo the grand staircase inside the home.

Along the home's south side, drifts of long-blooming blue-flowered Russian sage gently billow through the bars of the iron fencing. An endearing bronze statue of a playful young foal lies amidst drifts of purple fountain grass and Mexican feather grass *(Nasella tenuissima*, formerly *Stipa tenuissima)*, the soft strands moving in a gentle breeze like silky horsetails. A raised bed along the front of the house contains a neat row of tree-form Tardiva hydrangeas *(H. paniculata* 'Tardiva'), a late-blooming cultivar with long-lasting conical white flowers. Elegant vase-shaped 'Bloodgood' Japanese maples *(Acer palmatum* var. *atropurpureum)* continue along the stone pathway, their lacy burgundy foliage turning a glorious orange-red in fall. Even though the garden is relatively new, much of the home's formidable stone facade is already softened with Boston ivy.

A wide variety of annuals planted throughout the garden brings a bold splash of color all summer long. The color palette and plant varieties are changed each year for a fresh look. In 2008, the central color theme was red (one of the racetrack's official colors). Scarlet drifts of sun-loving New Guinea impatiens and petunias were planted along the front.

The side entrance to the Riggi garden. *Top:* Ornamental grasses provide a soft backdrop for a bronze statue of a reclining foal. *Middle:* Another bronze, of a mare and foal, stands in a more formal setting.

A statue of a mare and foal, the centerpiece of the northeast corner, was accented with adjacent urns spilling with red Calibrachoa and verbena with burgundy Cordyline.

The centerpiece of the front gardens consists of two impressive Italian stone fountains set on either side of the front entryway. Four greyhound statues, a nod to Michele's passion for dogs, stand guard at the base of the stairway. Michele keeps a real-life medley of thirty-one small canines, including chihuahuas, Yorkshire terriers, and Papillons, in a separate area on the property.

A narrow side pathway that leads to the backyard is planted on both sides in a mirror image. Eight vase-shaped European beech *(Fagus sylvatica* 'Rohanii') provide a shady canopy of rich purple foliage in spring that fades to bronze-green in summer. The trees are underplanted with clumps of exotic Egyptian papyrus *(Cyperus papyrus* 'King Tut'), their feathery plumes contrasting with an outline of neatly clipped boxwood hedges.

Because English boxwood, which is used liberally throughout the gardens, is marginally hardy in northern climates, Rich Morris uses several newer Korean hybrids bred for their winter hardiness. 'Green Gem' has a rounded habit, reaching just two feet by two feet at maturity; needs little trimming and is hardy to USDA Zone 4. 'Green Mountain' is a more vigorous grower with a columnar and upright habit; it is also hardy to USDA Zone 4. 'Green Velvet' has a dense, compact habit that is ideal for hedging. It is shade tolerant and slightly less hardy than the other two (USDA Zone 5).

Red was the prevailing accent color in the plantings at the Riggi entry garden in 2008. Two Italian fountains anchor the formal entry garden.

Behind the house, gently cascading waterfalls trickle down two levels to the main turquoise-hued swimming pool. To keep the overall design of the poolside pavilion from being too heavy, it was designed with a stucco finish of muted earth tones. The limestone used for the pavilion entryway arches was imported from the Yucatan Peninsula in Mexico. Standing sentinel at the pavilion entrance are two lion statues, obtained from the estate of former local entrepreneur and philanthropist Charles Wood.

A stone wall that runs across the rear of the property is punctuated with faux arched alcoves decorated with window boxes. A back garden is framed by an expanse of green lawn with a large reflecting pool and fountain as the focal point. Gracing the edge of the reflecting pool are stone planters and large urns set on pedestals. A bronze horse statue overlooks the water. Another nearby pool is home to large specimens of Japanese koi in brilliant white, orange, and black. Some of the fish are named, including Sir Winston, who is bright orange, and a pure white koi dubbed Moby Dick.

What is most remarkable about the house and gardens is the accessibility to passersby. The garden was deliberately designed to invite the gazes and glimpses of strolling neighbors and out-of-town visitors. The wrought-iron and stone fence is just high enough to afford the owners some privacy yet allow spectators to view the spectacular landscaping from the sidewalk. At the estate's southeast corner on the outside of the fence is a triangular welcome garden of formal boxwood woven into three interlocking hearts. The centers of the heart-shaped hedges are planted with scarlet coleus rimmed with silver dusty miller. Urns and planters grace the backdrop wall, which features the family monogram in gold surrounded by decorative iron swirls. Vintage-style street lamps along the curb are surrounded with island beds of bold crimson-leaved King Humbert canna lilies (C. x *generalis* 'King Humbert'), red coleus, purple fountain grass, scarlet amaranthus, red Million Bells, and contrasting chartreuse potato vine.

The Riggis, who are well known in the community, host a score of parties and charitable benefits during the summer. When they literally roll out the red carpet from the home's front entrance to the curb for one of their much-anticipated events, passing tourists stop to take photos of themselves on the scarlet walkway.

After the summer season wanes, the garden is decorated in harvest colors. Brightly hued pumpkins and gourds, bunches of dried cornstalks, and garlands of bittersweet are placed in artful combinations around the yard and atop the wall of the welcome garden. Summer annuals are replaced with red and yellow potted chrysanthemums. In late fall, the grounds are adorned with lights and decorations for the holiday season. During the long winter, plans for the upcoming growing season's landscape will be contemplated, and Saratoga's public will once again be treated to a street-side display by one of the city's most charismatic couples. ❧

Classic statuary adorns the Riggis' two-level pool, which is overlooked by a private pavilion.

In spring, the greenhouses at Dehn's burst with welcome color from impatiens, plumed cockscomb, and begonias. HISTORIC POSTCARD ON OPPOSITE PAGE COURTESY SARATOGA ROOM, SARATOGA LIBRARY

Our modern greenhouses directly adjoin this up-to-the-minute flower shop. Our facilities are unexcelled in Northern New York.

Business AND *Blooms*

Flower-related businesses have been a mainstay in Saratoga since the early days, yet most of the original florists and nurseries have come and gone. In 1875, John Ralph began selling roses, sweet peas, Easter lilies, and primroses for special occasions from his greenhouse on Woodlawn Avenue. Thomas J. Totten grew and sold roses and carnations in the early 1900s at his greenhouse on Nelson Avenue and ran a seasonal shop inside the Grand Union Hotel. And florist Henry Schrade, a fixture on Broadway beginning in the early 1900s, offered cut roses to smitten suitors for a dollar a dozen. These small horticultural enterprises left a lasting impression on the Spa City, making it a more beautiful place.

Five Generations

For more than a century, Dehn's Flowers & Greenhouses has not only survived but thrived. This iconic establishment opened in 1892 at its current location on Beekman Street, and today the garden center is run by fourth-generation owner Charles "Dude" Dehn, carrying on the tradition of his father and grandfather. Dude's great-grandfather Christian Dehn, who emigrated from Germany, started it all. He traveled to America in the early 1890s, hoping to land a job at the Chicago World's Fair. Arriving in New York Harbor, he heard of the mineral springs in Saratoga, which were reminiscent of those in his hometown. So instead of Chicago, Christian headed for Saratoga and settled in the working-class neighborhood of Dublin, a west-side enclave of small wood-frame homes, boarding houses, and family-run stores. He purchased a plot of land and opened a small shop, offering fresh flowers for sale.

Today, Dehn's full-service shop still carries cut flowers and also makes floral arrangements for holidays, weddings, and special occasions, including the many dinner parties and galas thrown during racing season, when track socialites are known to request custom arrangements made with their stable colors. The adjoining retail nursery offers a superb selection of annuals, perennials, vegetable starts, and shrubs in its large display area and twenty greenhouses spanning two city blocks.

Through two world wars and the Great Depression, and weathering Saratoga's own cycles of boom and bust, Dehn's nursery has decorated some of the city's most illustrious estates and commercial establishments. It was their job to brighten up the grand courtyard of the former Grand Union Hotel and plant two hundred feet of flower boxes along the veranda of the now-defunct United States Hotel. They landscaped many of the casinos that sprang up during Saratoga's gambling heyday, including Riley's, The Brook, and Newman's Lake House.

Dude recalls an incident that occurred at Piping Rock, one of the most popular casinos, located outside of town on Union Avenue. His grandfather planted the grounds for the summer tourist season, but the management wouldn't pay him. Finally, when the season was halfway through and he still hadn't been paid, he brought a crew of men armed with shovels and threatened to dig out all the plants and haul them away. He was fully compensated on the spot.

For nearly five decades, Dehn's has contracted to provide bedding plants for the 350-acre Saratoga Race Course grounds, growing most of the plants themselves and sending their own staff to put them in the ground. Dude's son-in-law, John Mishoe, who manages the greenhouses, installs many of the stable plantings ordered by trainers and horse owners. Flowers for a scene in the 1981 film *Ghost Story*, filmed in Saratoga, came from Dehn's. (The footage ultimately wound up on the cutting room floor.)

Dude, who has been at the helm since 1960, expects that his son-in-law will take over the reins of the family business. No matter what the future holds, it's safe to say that Dehn's Flowers will continue its long-standing tradition of helping to beautify a city whose love of flowers has similarly stood the test of time.

A Destination for All Seasons

Driving out Church Street, past the intersection with Western Avenue and the boundary that marks the transition between city and country, it's easy to miss the nursery that sits in the shadow of the overpass. Yet visitors who venture down the narrow entrance road are instantly transported into a quaint countryside setting

Sunnyside Gardens was opened by Ned and Bonnie Chapman in 1982 on property once used by the Schrade family's nursery business. Today, the Chapmans' operation has grown from two greenhouses to seventeen, offering a dazzling selection of hanging baskets, vegetables, annuals, perennials, rosebushes, and other landscape plants. Most of the annual bedding plants are grown from seeds, cuttings, and plugs (small plant starts) beginning in late winter. In addition to their busy walk-in traffic, Sunnyside supplies plants to the gardens at Yaddo, the Racino, the Fasig-Tipton auction grounds, and the estates of some of Saratoga's

Whimsical displays are part of the fun when Sunnyside Gardens sets up its annual Halloween Pumpkin Patch display.

summer residents. The Chapmans retain five or six full-time employees year-round, including their daughter Heather, increasing to twenty workers in summer.

One of Sunnyside's biggest clients is the city of Saratoga Springs, whose streets they have helped beautify since 2007. Ned Chapman works closely with the department of public works, growing plants to the city's specifications for flower beds and hanging baskets in Congress Park, on Broadway, and in other high-profile areas.

Sunnyside hosts special events throughout the season and weekly educational seminars in May. Garden clubs and other groups can request special tours of the nursery grounds.

It's obvious that the Chapmans like their customers to have fun. The nursery's biggest event is the Halloween Pumpkin Patch in October, when the front display area is decorated with bright orange pumpkins, multicolored gourds, cornstalks, hay bales, and "Monster Mums." Stuffed scarecrow figures and wooden cutout scenes provide whimsical backdrops where children (and young-at-heart adults) can pose for photos. A train with pint-size cars chugs along a track that loops around the outside of the displays, to the delight of its young passengers. During the week, the garden center welcomes visiting school groups, and on fair-weather weekends families line up for hayrides and a trip through the butterfly house. On the way out, they'll load up the car with basketball-size pumpkins and whimsically labeled "Monster Mums" for the trip home. Chapman has noticed parents who came here as children returning to create fun memories for their own kids.

For the owners of Sunnyside, giving back to the community and seeing their customers have fun are the aspects of their business they enjoy the most.

Farmers' Market Cornucopia

The summer Saratoga Farmers' Market, which celebrates its thirty-second year in 2010, is located on High Rock Avenue adjacent to the city's first-discovered mineral spring. Vendors offer a diverse array of products, including locally grown fruits and vegetables, fresh eggs, baked goods, berry jams, organic honey, maple syrup, artisanal cheeses, and nonfood items such as crafts and handmade soaps. Patrons are serenaded with live music and seduced by the aroma of freshly brewed coffee. The open-air covered venue features fifty vendors and is held rain or shine on Wednesdays and Saturdays from May until November. A smaller winter market is held indoors at the Division Street Elementary School.

From Farm to Market

As a child, Suzanne Balet Haight knew exactly what she wanted to do when she grew up. Raised on her family's homestead just south of Saratoga in the town of Malta, she was drawn to the earth's natural rhythms, the ebb and flow of the seasons that farmers depend on for their livelihoods. When she was eight years old, she began helping her mom at the Saratoga Farmers' Market, where the Balets were among the original vendors.

Despite her parents' reservations, Suzanne decided to pursue a career in horticulture. The fresh-faced woman with a sunny smile attended the State University of New York (SUNY) Cobleskill, continuing her education at Cornell University, where she received a bachelor's degree in ornamental horticulture and floriculture. She also learned the art of floral design. Upon graduation, Suzanne returned home to lease some of the family's acreage, growing bedding plants, herbs, cutting flowers, and vegetable seedlings.

In 1995, Suzanne returned to the Saratoga Farmers' Market under her own business name of Balet Flowers & Design, selling potted plants, seedlings, and freshly cut flowers. Her informal country-style bouquets earned rave reviews, so she expanded her business to provide floral arrangements for weddings and other special occasions. Her signature creations have graced regional establishments such as the Canfield Casino, the Hall of Springs, the Saratoga National Gol Course, and the renowned Sagamore Resort on Lake George.

In addition to selling cut flowers to a local wholesaler, Balet Flowers & Design continues to be a popular fixture at the farmers' market, selling cut flowers by the stem, arranged bouquets, and a medley of potted annuals and perennials out of the back of a large delivery truck.

Back on her family farm, Suzanne grows more than 150 varieties of annuals, 200 types of perennials, and a selection of vegetable starts and herbs on five acres. At the retail outlet on site, customers can cut their own bouquets from seemingly endless rows of sunflowers, amaranthus, spider flower, cockscomb, asters, marigolds, strawflowers *(Bracteantha)*, zinnias, and snapdragons. The gentle valley views, the musical birdsong, the spicy scent of marigolds, and the occasional frog nestled between the rows of blooms are captivating diversions as one browses among the potted plants and nursery stock displayed along several hoop houses.

Suzanne considers herself lucky to be doing what she loves and raising her two young children with her husband, David Haight, in the simple, wholesome lifestyle she grew up with. "I wouldn't have it any other way," she says.

Center: Suzanne Balet Haight's cut flowers are always popular at the Saratoga Farmers' Market. *Opposite:* Susan Johnson began her organization, Seeds for Peace, at her kitchen table.

Saratoga's Seed Lady

When Susan Johnson read an article in the local newspaper about homeless people in Bosnian refugee camps who were growing their own food, the lifelong gardener thought, why not send them some seeds? The idea germinated into a nonprofit organization called Seeds for Peace International, Inc., which Johnson runs single-handedly from her kitchen table. Her small apartment does extra duty as an office, warehouse, and packaging facility, where she sorts and repackages seeds that are donated or are bought as surplus from seed companies at a deep discount.

The seeds are shipped to such faraway places as Uganda, Tanzania, Namibia, South Africa, Paraguay, El Salvador, and Guatemala. Many of the African recipients are AIDS orphans and widows. In Lesotho, a small independent country surrounded by the larger nation of South Africa, orphans are able to feed themselves from food grown from Johnson's donated seeds. Surplus harvest is sold at a local market, and the proceeds are used to purchase essentials such as soap, candles, and toothpaste.

The biggest recipient of Seeds for Peace is Bosnia-Herzegovina, where the seeds are distributed by the American Friends Service Committee (AFSC). In 2007, Johnson sent nearly 2,900 seed packets, which were distributed to fourteen community gardens in this war-torn eastern European nation.

Seeds for Peace has extended a helping hand in the United States as well, shipping seeds to residents of Mississippi, some of whom were affected by Hurricane Katrina.

The AFSC and other beneficiaries of the program have e-mailed Susan photos of the people she's helped: families often pictured next to their crops of carrots, onions, lettuce, potatoes, cabbage, beets, corn, peppers, and various herbs. Putting a face on world hunger and seeing the results of her efforts make Johnson's mission more personal. She uses these powerful images in talks she gives at public schools, Rotary clubs, and church groups, and the Saratoga community has responded with volunteer help and donations. Area nurseries and hardware stores also pitch in, donating seeds left over from the previous growing season. Susan's boundless energy and tireless efforts have earned her the nickname of "the Seed Lady."

As the name Seeds for Peace suggests, Susan's mission goes beyond growing food. In places such as Bosnia where there is ethnic strife, the gardens provide a haven where people can set aside their differences and share their common interest of growing food. Her organization's motto, "Changing the world, one garden at a time," reflects her goal of expanding the program to aid more people in all parts of the world.

Johnson's two children pitch in to help. Sam Cherubin, who was born in 1998, the year Johnson started her project, and Anna Cherubin, who was born two years earlier, cannot remember a time when their mother was not helping others. The children sort seeds and prepare boxes for shipping, often tucking in stuffed animals, chocolate, greeting cards, and plastic hand tools to round out the care packages. They've already learned a valuable life lesson about helping others.

Between raising her children, working as a fitness trainer and a seasonal garden designer, and running her organization, Johnson has little time to tend to her own yard. Fortunately, her tiny plot consists of an assortment of hostas and other low-maintenance perennials. Even though she has little free time, she says the sacrifice is worth it. "All I have to do is look at photos of the people I'm helping, and it keeps me going," she says.

In 2008, Johnson traveled to Bosnia and Croatia, where she was able to meet some of the people she's helped and to see firsthand the results of her efforts. Though many of the people she met had little in material possessions, they opened their homes and their hearts. Johnson's unwavering enthusiasm and sense of purpose in helping people to feed themselves prove the old adage that one person really can make a difference in the world.

"Old Professor's" Daylilies

Daylilies are a staple of northern gardens, and few people knew this better than Dr. Stanley Saxton. A music professor at Skidmore College for forty years, Saxton taught piano and organ until his retirement in 1965. One of Saxton's lesser-known passions was gardening. He first began growing flowers during the 1930s at his family's summer camp at Tupper Lake in the Adirondacks, where winter temperatures can plunge to –40 degrees Fahrenheit. When he had little success overwintering plants, he began to notice the orange daylilies (*Hemerocallis fulva*), planted long ago by homesteaders and still thriving along the backcountry roads.

Saxton sought out other daylilies that would survive the harsh winters, visiting growers around the East Coast in search of the sturdiest varieties. He learned how to hybridize the lilies, a process of crossbreeding that involves fertilizing the ovary of one variety with the pollen of another. The resulting seed is then used to grow new plants, with the hope that the resulting seedlings will display the desired traits from both parents. From germination to bloom, the process takes at least two years. Saxton's efforts resulted in a series of cold-hardy varieties he called the Adirondack Strain, which he shared with gardener friends. In addition to winter hardiness, other characteristics Dr. Saxton deemed desirable were good branching (resulting in more blooms) and the ability to rebloom.

What started as a beloved hobby became a thriving seasonal business. Saxton continued to amass an extensive daylily collection, growing hundreds of varieties in neat rows on an acre of land at his First Street property and keeping meticulous records. Eventually he began selling

the plants to local gardeners. He published his first catalog in 1943 and cultivated a wide following among daylily enthusiasts around the country. His daylilies were also sold commercially by prominent national companies such as Park Seed. Saxton was a founding member of the American Hemerocallis Society, and more than three hundred Saxton varieties have been registered with that prestigious association.

Daylilies are valued because they will thrive in a wide range of climates and conditions. Many varieties reliably make it through the long Saratoga winters (USDA Zones 4b to 5a). They come in nearly every color imaginable except blue and white, and sizes from miniature to large (eight and a half inches or more across). The blooms take many different forms, including ruffled, spider, trumpet, recurved, and double. Each individual flower lasts just one day, hence the name. Depending on the variety, bloom time ranges from early summer well into fall. Some, such as 'Stella de Oro', are repeat bloomers, flowering for months on end.

Known affectionately as "the Old Professor," Saxton passed away in 2002 at the age of ninety-seven. He was joined in the daylily business by his son Peter in 1970. A mechanical draftsman by trade, Peter turned to learning the daylily business from the ground up. He has created hybrid varieties both on his own and jointly with his father.

Dr. Saxton took great pleasure in naming varieties after people he knew. 'Twila Wolfe' was named for a former student who was crowned Miss North Dakota in 1960. She now sells real estate in Montana, and gives her namesake plant as a housewarming gift each time she sells a home. 'Doris Myrna' was named after his sister, and a fellow daylily society member named Mildred Bradley was also honored with her own variety. Other cultivars were named for Adirondack locales: 'Saranac Snowflake', 'Lake Placid', and 'Ausable Gold'. The Saxton father-and-son team honored their hometown as well, with names such as 'Saratoga Strutter', 'Saratoga Redcoat', and 'Saratoga Concerto', a nod to Dr. Saxton's love of music.

In 2010, Saxton Gardens celebrates its sixty-seventh year in business. Peter continues to produce a small printed catalog in an age where most nurseries conduct business solely over the Internet. He prints a thousand catalogs annually, mailing out four hundred to regular customers. He receives orders from all fifty states as well as England and Australia. Ninety-five percent of his business is mail order, though he still has a small walk-in clientele.

During the growing season, Peter often can be found in the garden from early morning until dark. He cherishes his simple lifestyle and eschews modern technology, answering the phone only when he's not busy dividing plants or filling orders. He prefers the old-fashioned way of doing business: personal contact, repeat customers, and word of mouth. In a world consumed by technology and rife with anonymity, his customers find his approach both charming and refreshing. Because gardening itself allows one to slow down and connect with nature, Saxton's approach to his business and life in general go hand in hand.

Many hardy daylily cultivars have been developed at Saxton Gardens on First Street, among them 'Saratoga Strutter' *(top right)* and 'Saratoga Pinwheel', *(lower left)*.

Keeping It in the Family

One of Saratoga's oldest continuously operated florists is Schrade's Posie Peddler on Congress Street. Henry Schrade, who emigrated to the United States from Germany, visited Saratoga for the floral fêtes in the 1890s and ended up settling here. Before opening his own florist shop in 1910, he created flower displays for the House of Pansa, a nineteenth-century reproduction of an ancient Pompeian villa, and worked for Charles Dehn at a property on Clark Street, the site of the present-day of Five Corners. Schrade's Flowers, which was the first year-round florist establishment in downtown Saratoga, originally was located on the corner of Broadway and Spring Street, with greenhouses and a separate store on Nelson Avenue adjacent to the thoroughbred racetrack.

Schrade's Flowers hopscotched across Broadway two times, relocating in 1924 to the Arcade Building a few blocks north (the present site of Prudential Manor), then to the Adelphi Hotel building (where Maestro's Restaurant is now). When Schrade began spending winters in Florida due to his health, he also opened florist shops in Palm Beach (managed by his brother Karl) and West Palm Beach. His business was the first in Florida to be affiliated with FTD, the professional florists' organization. The family business expanded further when Schrade opened a shop at the Queensbury Hotel in Glens Falls, New York, managed by his son Henry, Jr.

Schrade kept records of his longtime customers, some of whom split their time between Florida and Saratoga. The list reads like a who's who of the era: Mr. and Mrs. E. F. Hutton, Babe Ruth, Samuel Riddle (owner of the legendary horse Man o' War), Chauncey Olcott, President Warren G. Harding, Mrs. Woodrow Wilson, Mrs. Franklin D. Roosevelt, Charles E. Schwab, Elizabeth Arden, Irving Berlin, and members of several royal families. His journal records decades' worth of special events, including May Day, Easter, Skidmore College dances, senior balls, and class days. An undated ad in the local newspaper for Memorial Day advertised peonies, gladioli, carnations, and mixed bouquets for a dollar, blooming plants starting at ten cents, and cemetery urns for four dollars.

In 1901, William Whitney offered Henry Schrade eight thousand dollars to buy some of the land he owned adjacent to the track. Henry accepted the offer, and the parcel became what is now the paddock, where the horses are promenaded and the jockeys are mounted before a race.

Henry Schrade, Jr., became mayor of the city of Saratoga Springs and was appointed foreman of a crew that helped build the New Spa complex at the Saratoga Reservation (now part of Saratoga Spa State Park). He was put in charge of tree removal and trimming and general landscaping. The New Spa became internationally renowned for its facilities, where patrons could bathe or ingest the spring waters to treat a wide array of maladies. Schrade's shop in Glens Falls was eventually closed, as were the stores in Florida, possibly wiped out by a hurricane.

Henry Sr.'s son William continued the family business on Broadway, but he eventually tore down the greenhouses on Nelson Avenue. The original home is still in the family and is now operated as a bed-and-breakfast by Judy Schrade (www.spa.net/schrade). Paul

Schrade, William's son, recalls a rural lifestyle on the Nelson Avenue property, where his family put food on the table during the Great Depression by raising chickens and growing their own fruits and vegetables. His mother's family owned a bakery in Poughkeepsie and shipped huge boxes of baked goods to the Schrades in Saratoga.

Paul worked in the family's nursery business, too, before going to college to study chemistry. Returning to Saratoga, he interned at the Simon Baruch Research Laboratory in the Spa Reservation, where he tested the mineral spring waters for various properties. Eventually Paul moved to California and chose a different vocation, but he still maintains a garden.

In 1974, William's son Jack and his wife, Nancy, started their own shop on Broadway called the Posie Peddler. They also set up a greenhouse operation on Church Street at the present-day site of Sunnyside Gardens. After finishing school and apprenticing at a Schenectady florist, their daughter Gretchen returned to carry on the family tradition at Posie Peddler. In 1978, she purchased the Posie Peddler from her father, and had bought out her grandfather seven years later, consolidating both stores in 1996. Schrade's Posie Peddler operated on Broadway until 2005, when it moved to its present location in Congress Plaza. The sidewalk entrance of the quaint shop, which Gretchen operates with her husband, Jim Squires, is decorated with colorful bouquets and plants. Inside the well-kept store is a walk-in cooler where customers can select their own flowers. The European-style display includes more than seventy-five types of flowers set on rotating shelves so that visitors can view arrangements and bouquets up close. The shop also offers custom arrangements and flowers for weddings and other special occasions.

Although its location and storefront displays have changed over the years, Schrade's has a hundred-year history of supplying floral displays to Saratogians.

HISTORIC PHOTO COURTESY OF GRETCHEN SCHRADE SQUIRES

For Gretchen, continuing the family business was in her blood. Though she studied other agricultural subjects in college, such as soil science and growing farm crops, she inevitably gravitated back to the retail floral trade. The business she's worked hard to build over the years would make her great-grandfather proud. ⚜

Gardens IN *Town*

Honoring a Timeless Tradition

When Suzanne Birdsall and her husband, Max, purchased their Walnut Street home in 1980, they had no idea they were also acquiring a bit of Saratoga's history. Their west-side location in the heart of the Dublin district is a neighborhood of modest wood-structure homes and storefronts settled first by Irish laborers hired for the booming building industry during the 1830s and then by the Italian masons, bricklayers, and stonecutters who followed in the 1880s. The new Italian residents established a section called Little Italy, opening small shops that sold groceries and hard goods and offered services such as shoe repair and barbering.

The Birdsalls' home, built around 1870, was once occupied by an Italian family who built a chicken coop out back and grew several kinds of grapes on a large arbor. A carefully tended vegetable plot produced bushels of tomatoes, peppers, and other vegetables used in their native cuisine. Large pots of marinara sauce were slowly simmered for hours over a cookstove in the garage, then ladled into glass preserving jars for the winter. Some of the grapes were used to make homemade wine, which won raves from the neighbors.

The Birdsalls, who had previously lived on a ten-acre rural property, wanted to re-create the seclusion and bucolic scenery of their former country home in their new 50 by 150-foot lot. They kept the existing vegetable garden and ninety-year-old Concord grape vines, and eventually Suzanne began to expand the gardens, creating "rooms" that served separate

Right: A Tuscan-inspired garden room at the rear of the Birdsall garden offers a private retreat. *Above:* Flower boxes bring color to the front porch. The cutout-pattern apron below the porch was made by Suzanne Birdsall's brother-in-law.

functions. Relying more on instinct than on formal design techniques, she created a landscape that suited her individual taste. The different areas make the garden feel larger than it is, encouraging viewers to stop and notice small elements they might normally overlook. Suzanne enjoys the element of surprise and mystery that each new vista offers.

For privacy, the entire backyard is enclosed by a six-foot-tall fence and an arborvitae hedge. Over the years, Suzanne has trained a diverse collection of vines up the weathered cedar fence, including hardy kiwi *(Actinidia)*, roses, chocolate vine *(Akebia quinata)*, and American bittersweet *(Celastrus scandens)*. She reports that the latter two have proven to be somewhat aggressive, so they must be used judiciously even by gardeners in colder zones.

Suzanne embraced the idea of incorporating recycled materials into the landscape long before it became fashionable. An iron gate rescued from an alleyway is now used as a trellis. Brick salvaged from an excavated sidewalk on Clinton Street forms the meandering pathway that replaced a straight cement sidewalk. Extending from the back porch to a garage at the rear of the property, the brick path links all the individual garden rooms. The pale terra-cotta-colored trim on the house echoes the tone of the salvaged brick, and splashes of scarlet blooms throughout the garden echo the house's primary color of deep red.

In spring, the garden comes alive with flowering dogwood, redbud *(Cercis canadensis)*, serviceberry *(Amelanchier)*, and crabapple *(Malus)*, with an understory of azaleas and the ground cover sweet woodruff *(Galium odoratum)*. The covered back porch, a cool place to sit on warm summer days, opens onto a series of cottage-style borders. The beds, which reach peak bloom in July, are filled with long-blooming perennials, such as astilbe, purple loosestrife *(Lythrum salicaria)*, daylilies, hosta, iris, cranesbill geraniums, bugbane *(Cimicifuga)*, and lady's mantle *(Alchemilla mollis)*. A wooden bench sits beside a bluestone patio made from pieces of an old cistern excavated from the backyard. Stands of paper birch placed at occasional intervals offer focal points, leading visitors down the brick walkway. Large-leaved hostas in complementary colors of blue and chartreuse further anchor the borders.

In the formal herb garden, a cement birdbath seems to float above drifts of lavender. The marble tiles surrounding the circular lavender bed were salvaged from a neighbor's home-improvement project. The soothing sound of cascading water emanates from a nearby water garden constructed on the site of the former chicken coop. The banks of the small pond, lined with river rock, are lushly planted with shade-tolerant cranesbill geraniums, ostrich ferns *(Matteuccia struthiopteris)*, hydrangea, and bee balm, evoking the feel of a natural bog in the Adirondack woods. Variegated hostas and iris with creamy white-and-green–striped foliage brighten the deeply shaded area. Hardy waterlilies *(Nymphaea)*, arrowhead *(Sagittaria)*, floating water hyacinth *(Eichhornia crassipes)*, and other aquatic plants thrive in the shallow water.

At the end of the brick pathway is a secluded seating area underneath the grapevines, where the Birdsalls often spend time reading or enjoying an evening meal. Here Suzanne has skillfully incorporated the garage and an adjoining shed to create a Tuscan-style backdrop that honors the previous occupants. The walls are painted a cream color with a warm terra-cotta trim to echo the brick patio. The garage windows are decorated with lacy

Above: Daisies and tickseed fill a perennial bed behind a garden bench and decades-old grapevines shade the garden room backed by the garage. *Right:* A pathway of mellow-colored brick links all the outdoor rooms in the Birdsall garden. A crabapple and an azalea offer shades of pink in the spring.

curtains and forest green shutters salvaged from a neighboring home, giving the appearance of an Italian villa. Large vase-shaped ferns planted at the garage's foundation add to the Mediterranean feel.

As is typical in the center of town, the soil on the Birdsalls' city lot is loamy sand. Suzanne keeps soil amendments simple and organic, applying a dressing of cow manure and bonemeal, which is a slow-release source of phosphorus. Bark mulch placed around acid-loving rhododendrons and azaleas conserves moisture and helps maintain the lower-pH environment these shrubs prefer.

For Suzanne and Max, the nearly thirty years they have invested in creating their urban Eden have more than paid off. The amount of time they spend in their yard in summer and the enjoyment it brings are probably just what their Italian predecessors had in mind.

A Best-dressed Garden

Decorating Saratoga's elegant homes and quintessential hostelries is a personal calling for Michele Erceg, owner of Best Dressed Windows In Town (www.bestdressedwindowsintown.com). Her life took some turns before landing her in the Spa City and her dream career. As a child, Erceg loved to sew, and she later studied to become a home economics teacher. On a whim, the New Jersey native, fresh out of college, answered a call for stewardesses for Eastern Airlines. She came to the interview attired in one of her snappiest handmade tailored suits and was hired on the spot.

As she flew to destinations around the United States, Erceg kept her eyes open for a place to call home. A trip to Saratoga Springs (where a new beau lived) convinced her to put down roots here. The quaint downtown, Victorian architecture, and sense of community were just what she was looking for. Erceg bought a Queen Anne–style cottage, built for a racing jockey in 1884, on one of Saratoga's east side streets. After renovating the home's interior, she turned her attention to the outside.

She had the gingerbread facade painted in three shades of pink to match the flowers of an old-fashioned Peegee hydrangea at the house's southwest corner. A handcrafted gable carving adorned with a gold swan and the family name, made by Erceg's father, holds great sentimental value. The intricate detailing was inspired by a visit to Eureka, California, known for its historic Victorian mansions, called "painted ladies."

Erceg planted perennial borders on her tiny city lot, built window boxes and filled them with colorful flowers, and hung baskets of blooming annuals along the front porch. She enjoyed adorning her home with freshly cut bouquets, but was dissatisfied with the

Clockwise from top left:
The gingerbread facade of Michele Erceg's house is as cheerful and bright as the flower beds around it. Adirondack chairs invite the garden visitor to pause and enjoy a sublime summer evening at The Farm. Even the hitching post outside Erceg's house is gaily decorated.

resulting loss of color in the garden. When a property across the street went up for sale, Erceg and her husband immediately made an offer. Erceg created extensive cutting gardens and a vegetable plot on the new property, which she whimsically named The Farm.

Erceg's schedule with the airline left her large blocks of free time, so she set up a part-time sewing business out of her home, offering custom-made drapes, slipcovers, bedspreads, dust ruffles, and window treatments. When Eastern Airlines went out of business in the mid-1980s, she relaunched her business full-time. As her reputation for creating fine furnishings grew, she was hired to decorate some of Saratoga's finest mansions and notable establishments.

The gardens around her house now include curbside plantings of long-blooming daylilies, coneflower, sedums, and black-eyed Susan. The vibrant flower beds set against the backdrop of the home's quaint facade draws regular compliments from neighbors and passersby. At The Farm, Erceg focuses on raising her favorite cutting flowers: spring-blooming peonies, sunflowers and giant zinnias for summer, and multihued chrysanthemums for fall. The peonies do double-duty providing greenery in bouquets, as Erceg prefers their long-lasting foliage to the more traditional ferns. She grows the zinnias in regular-size tomato cages to prevent the stems from bending or breaking in the inevitable summer cloudbursts.

Though she isn't much of a cook, Erceg grows a bevy of tomatoes, a skill passed down to her from her father. Her mother taught her to preserve the crop into savory winter sauces, a tradition she still honors each harvest season. Standard tomato cages bend over from the weight of her hefty vines, so she fashions her own wire cylinders from four-inch-gauge fencing. The sturdy supports are economical to make and last over many seasons, and she can easily reach in through the mesh to pick the fruits. Her other favorite vegetable-growing indulgence is a medley of brightly colored ornamental gourds, which wind up as decorations for the Thanksgiving table.

Erceg has developed other money-saving gardening methods. A favorite plant for her window boxes is golden creeping Jenny, with its raindrop-like golden foliage dripping down from the planters like a warm summer shower. In fall, she digs the plants out of the boxes and heels them into raised beds at The Farm to overwinter, then replants them in the boxes next spring. She peruses local garden centers for four-inch pots of chrysanthemums left from the previous year, reasoning that if they have made it through the winter, they must be the hardiest specimens. To retain their bushy habit, Erceg cuts the mums back in May and June, dips the cut stems in Rootone (a growth hormone), and inserts them into the ground next to the mother plant. Kept well watered, the cuttings will then develop into healthy new plants.

A wooden lattice fence Erceg built in the late 1980s fell apart in a windstorm in 2007. When the fence was rebuilt, she added a raised bed along its entire length. There are also two-foot-high raised beds at The Farm, and Erceg plans to eventually transition the rest of the garden to raised beds, which spare the gardener from having to do so much bending and kneeling. They also tend to warm up more quickly in spring, helping plants to grow faster. Erceg, who looks forward to many more years of gardening, cheerfully remarks, "I hope I'm still doing this in my eighties."

A Curbside Flower Bouquet

For those who drive along East Avenue in summer, Betsy Delay's yard is hard to miss. Long borders along her fence and around her home burst with color all season long. The property, a short drive north of the track, is a familiar sight to race goers and attendees at the nearby yearling auction who drive by during the season, and it's not unusual for strangers to stop and ask about the garden.

Delay has lived here for forty-five years with her husband, Walter, and gardened for thirty of those. She prefers to do things "her way" and doesn't subscribe to hard-and-fast rules found in many gardening books. She strives for bold color and a proliferation of blooms over the entire growing season. "I want the garden to look like one big flower bouquet," she says.

She plans for a grand burst of color in late spring. One of Delay's favorite flowers is sweet william, which she grows from seed sown the previous year. The old-fashioned flowers remind her of her grandmother and mother, both gardeners, and of days gone by. She plants twenty flats of seedlings, giving many of the starts to friends and family. The rest she plants into her garden in the fall so they'll give a burst of color the following May and June. Once they've finished blooming, she replaces them with annual zinnias and marigolds, which fill in the gaps around reliable perennials such as daylilies, black-eyed Susan, yarrow, bulbous lilies, bee balm, daisies, sedums, and cranesbill geraniums.

Delay's first daylilies came from the nearby Saxton gardens. More recently, she has acquired others from North Country Daylilies in Buskirk (www.northcountrydaylilies. com). Her collection now numbers several dozen varieties, including 'Adirondack Trust', named for the locally owned bank where she worked in the 1970s and 1980s. Now retired, she still fondly recalls her ten years there.

The well-established borders are amended with compost and topsoil as needed. Each spring, Delay feeds the perennials with 5-10-5 all-purpose fertilizer. She keeps the annuals blooming with water-soluble Miracle-Gro applied twice during the summer. The intensive planting method she uses means few gaps between the plants and, hence, few weeds.

Her newest border runs along the north side of the house. She experimented with many sun-loving perennials and was surprised at how well they did in the partially shaded space. The long, narrow bed of bee balm, daylilies, purple loosestrife, delphinium, queen-of-the-prairie *(Filipendula rubra)*, and balloon flower *(Platycodon grandiflorus)* is just as lush with blooms as the rest of the yard.

In late summer, Delay picks up gallon-size plants in full bloom on sale at local nurseries and uses them to fill gaps where other flowers have waned. This easy color supplement keeps the beds looking good to the end of the season.

Evenings are when Delay most enjoys puttering around, pinching off a dead blossom here and propping up a leaning plant there. It's a process she finds relaxing. She loves it when passersby comment on the garden. "I've met some of the nicest people because of my flowers," she says. Those who come by and enjoy the garden feel equally enriched.

Welcome to the Porch

Few things signify the past American way of life more than porches. These outdoor rooms were an important gathering place for family and friends. During the heyday of Saratoga's great hotels, patrons congregated on spacious verandas to socialize.

Today, Saratogians still participate in these friendly rituals, whether to sit for a glass of wine with friends before heading over to SPAC for the symphony, or to bask in the scents, sounds, and sights of a warm summer evening. Many of the city's homes have quaint porches, and people enjoy dressing them up with hanging baskets and small gardens in front.

Above: Exuberant blooms screen Jim and Joann Grande's porch on Union Avenue.

Top and left: Betsy Delay says she strives to make her densely planted flowerbeds look like "one big flower bouquet." *Above:* 'Adirondack Trust' is one of Delay's favorite daylilies.

The porch of Robb and Caroline Baker's east side house is adorned with hanging baskets, ferns, and elephant's ear. The cheerful blue home on East Avenue belongs to Betsy Delay's niece and neighbor, Joanne Zabala.

Ivy and impatiens decorate a topiary pony in Natalie Walsh's compact in-town garden. *Inset photos:* The quaint carriage house is a backdrop to the poolside gardens. Grate detail in the backyard garden gate.

A Garden to Write About

As the garden columnist for *The Daily Gazette* in Schenectady, Natalie Walsh tries to educate her readers about growing plants. It's a role that she relishes and meets with gusto when reporting on her latest horticulture endeavors. Her small urban Saratoga garden is the testing ground for the subjects she writes about. Topics ranging from easy-to-grow vegetables to the best-tasting tomato are often driven by her readers. She has developed a loyal following and an almost symbiotic relationship, where she shares with her readers the dizzying array of horticultural challenges and triumphs that each new season brings, and they respond in kind.

Walsh, who has a master's degree in journalism, freelanced out of her home while she raised her son. When he was older, she trained as a Master Gardener through Saratoga County and enjoyed it so much that she went back to school at SUNY Cobleskill for an associate's degree in floriculture. She approached the *Gazette* and was hired in 1998 to write a weekly gardening column that runs from early spring until Halloween. In 2005, Walsh was hired full-time as a special-sections editor.

After her son went off to college, Walsh and her husband, George, who lived in the southern Saratoga County town of Rexford, began searching for a country property where they could have a large garden and a fruit orchard. When they were unable to find what they were looking for, a friend suggested a house for sale in Saratoga. Though it didn't fit their need for space, the house more than made up for it in charm and location.

Located near the Fasig-Tipton yearling auction yards, the residence is typically Saratoga in style, a Victorian wood frame structure built in 1882. One of the more illustrious past occupants was Cora Mott, a cofounder of the Young Women's Industrial Club, which would later become Skidmore College. The narrow alleyway lined with carriages houses in back was once used by the horses and buggies of a bygone era.

Walsh's new house and small fenced yard were both in need of repair. While the house was being remodeled, the entire backyard was covered with black plastic to smother the bishop's weed that had taken over the space. After two full seasons, the house remodel was well along and the weeds were gone. The carriage house, which was renovated and painted beige and cream with brick-red trim to match the house, provides a quaint backdrop to the gardens.

Each year Walsh chooses a theme for her garden and writes about it in her column. Past topics have included growing small fruits (blueberries and strawberries) and salad greens (lettuces in a medley of colors and textures, ruffled and speckled; mesclun mix; tender dandelion leaves; and robust beet greens). Herbs are a favorite subject. Walsh has explored with her readers the use of herbs combined with edible flowers and greens for brightly colored salads.

Walsh enjoys throwing impromptu gatherings for friends and neighbors to share the fruits of her labor. Over several years, she hosted a taste-off for attendees to sample some twenty varieties of home-grown tomatoes. The winners included three heirlooms: 'Sophie's Choice', an early variety from Canada; 'Green Zebra', a striped fruit that tastes mild and sweet; and 'Large Pink Bulgarian', a beefsteak type with an intense, old-fashioned flavor.

Perhaps the most fun was a "bartender's garden," grown in 2008. Walsh experimented with combinations of basil, mint, lemon balm, rosemary, and thyme, creating cocktails with a small splash of liquor, or refreshing nonalcoholic drinks such as basil lemonade. The aptly named 'Kentucky Colonel' spearmint *(Mentha spicata)*, a staple of the mint julep beverages traditionally served at the Kentucky Derby, is a favorite herb for its sweet, flavorful leaves. Walsh invited friends over to sample the concoctions; two recipes—a beverage and a refreshing herb and fruit sorbet—were shared with her readers in a later column.

In 2006, the Walshes added an inground swimming pool, landscaping the western edge with a hedge of Quick Fire hydrangeas *(H. paniculata* 'Quick Fire') and an underplanting of lady's mantle. The hydrangea flowers, which start out white, fade to a color that Walsh describes as "baked apple," echoing the shade of beige on the main house and the carriage house. Classic urns and large ceramic pots placed around the pool area are planted with combinations that change yearly. Boldly colored Million Bells, petunias, annual geranium, coleus, and sweet potato vine are mixed with edibles such as sorrel *(Rumex sanguineus)*, tarragon, and basil.

Walsh puts every bit of available space in her tiny backyard to good use, working with the varying light conditions. A deeply shaded area off the back porch is planted with red impatiens, which brighten the space. A horse-shaped topiary obtained at the Philadelphia Flower Show provides a whimsical focal point. Walsh draped a plastic vertical grow bag over the horse's withers and planted it with red impatiens. The crimson "saddle" was reminiscent of the flower blankets traditionally placed on the winning horse at major stakes races.

An unexpected benefit of the house's location is its proximity to the Fasig-Tipton grounds. Walsh looks forward to the start of the two-week yearling auction each year, when a parade of horses, assorted tack, and flower baskets are unloaded from huge semitrailers, transforming the grounds overnight. The sights, sounds, and smells are unforgettable: the high whinnies of the young steeds as they receive their morning bath, the neatly planted beds of impatiens and the colorful containers hung along the front of the stables, and the intense scrutiny of prospective buyers who plunk down huge sums of money on the unproven equines. A summer filled with flowers, friends, and horses is a tonic that suits Walsh just fine.

A Healing Garden

For some people, gardening becomes part of their life in a most unexpected way. Mona Neubert was encouraged by friends to grow flowers long before she actually started, but the thought of getting her hands dirty didn't have much appeal. She made an attempt at raising indoor houseplants, but they usually died, reinforcing her self-perception of having a "black thumb."

When she and her husband, Christopher, moved to their present home in 2001, Neubert finally had a yard big enough for a garden. But her keen interest in interior design led her to remodel the home's inside first. Her love of Victorian style influenced the masterful redecoration of the vintage 1865 home with elaborate drapes, classic furniture, richly colored wallpaper, and other adornments.

Clockwise from lower left:
"Miss Mona" in the Neuberts'
shade garden. The small
side garden brims with color.
The welcoming front porch
overlooks an artfully planted
postage-stamp front yard. In
back, a hydrangea shades a
private seating area on the
back patio.

Once the inside of the home was finished, Neubert turned her attention to the yard. She was reluctant to do the work herself, but hiring someone else was out of the question. She finally began digging in the dirt, and this seemingly simple act was an epiphany; she instantly fell in love with the feel and smell of the soil. The anticipation of nurturing and watching the plants grow held equal appeal. A deeply spiritual person, she was at once affected with the connection she felt to the cycle of life that occurs in a garden.

Neubert immersed herself in gardening books and catalogs, absorbing all of the knowledge she could. She began experimenting with a wide range of perennials, annuals, and shrubs, from old standbys to the latest varieties. At first, she focused on plants for their blooms; later, as she learned more and the garden evolved, she tended toward varieties for their texture, foliage, and structure.

The garden awakens in early spring with the minor bulbs snow-drop and crocus, giving way to daffodils, tulips, and perennial hel-lebores *(Helleborus orientalis)*. Lilacs, white Japanese snowball vibur-num *(V. plicatum)*, and the delicate pink blooms of flowering almond *(Prunus glandulosa 'Rosa Plea')* offer a soft backdrop to perennial col-umbine, lungwort, and windflower *(Anemone)*. A favorite shrub is a newer Midnight Wine cultivar of weigela *(W. florida* 'Elvera') with deep purple foliage and hot pink blooms in spring. The dwarf variety, which matures at just twelve to eighteen inches tall and wide, is a good choice as a ground cover or an accent for small gardens.

Modest Mussorgsky's masterpiece symphony *Pictures at an Exhibi-tion* became a metaphor for the garden. The individual movements of the piano suite were meant to commemorate the artwork of the Rus-sian composer's close friend Viktor Hartmann, who died at a young age. Neubert viewed each section of her yard as a similar unique work of art, a blank canvas on which she could create inspired vignettes with plants and ornamentation.

Neubert's mother, with whom she was very close, passed away in 2007. The yard became a sanctuary and place of healing, and evolved into a tribute to her mother, who was also an avid gardener. Each new bloom became a symbol of the natural cycle of life, of birth and death. With Neubert's occupation as a critical-care nurse at Saratoga Hospital, this deeper manifestation of the garden was all the more poignant.

Neubert's passion for Victorian style is evident throughout the garden. The front porch, a backdrop to the curbside entry garden, is ornately painted in subtle shades of green, red, and cream. Scal-loped brick edging and a small iron fence enclose a deeply shaded bed rimmed with formal boxwoods and topiaried spruce. Saratoga-style urns on pedestals, a pineapple-topped fountain, and small lion statues complete the framework for the understated plantings of coleus, bego-nias, plectranthus *(P. argentatus* 'Aureo-marginata'), and green-leaved hosta. Comfortable wicker seats with striped cushions provide a place to relax on the porch. A garden adjacent to the driveway is similarly formal, with a black iron fence as a backdrop and a cherub statue as the focal point. Evergreen topiaries are interspersed with coleus, begonias, and hanging baskets of red salvia, Million Bells, potato vine, and dracaena.

A Greco-Roman–style maiden figurine, the centerpiece of the backyard shade garden, was purchased with a gift certificate from Neubert's nursing colleagues. Neubert wanted to honor those same people who originally encouraged her to garden, so she named the statue Miss Mona, her nickname at work. The shaded bed is home to a bright dis-play of begonias and impatiens, punctuated with the occasional variegated lungwort and white-leaved caladium. An elegant Victorian-style palm, the backdrop for Miss Mona, is replaced each year.

A cottage-style border on the north side of the house is packed with brightly colored flowers planted in a less formal style. Here Neubert can experiment with new varieties. Round mirrors along the fence and a reflecting aqua gazing globe make the narrow area feel more spacious. Small sconces of Bonfire begonias (*B. boliviensis* 'Bonfire') hung along the fence produce tendrils of fiery orange blooms all summer long. Newer varieties of Diamond Frost spurge (*Euphorbia* 'Diamond Frost') and Coconut Lime coneflower (*Echinacea purpurea* 'Coconut Lime') are interspersed with reliable standbys of peonies, lilies, bee balm, iris, and phlox.

A small rose border contains climbing 'Benjamin Britton' and 'Mary Rose' varieties of David Austin roses. Neubert favors the newer long-blooming Knock Out roses, which have proved to be reliable performers in the North Country. Lipstick red rose hips, which form after the flowers fade, last well into winter, offering beautiful contrast in newly fallen snow. Roses and clematis vines are a classic garden combination, and Neubert has several hardy clematis, including 'Henryi', 'Etoile Violette', and 'Josephine', growing among the roses.

The back deck is adorned with wicker chairs and cushions that match those on the front porch. Delicate porcelain figurines are accented by a backdrop of Peegee hydrangeas. Just off the deck is a small area dedicated to the Neuberts' young grandson. A child-size chair offers him a place to sit while he eagerly digs in the dirt. A small cherub birdbath and a cast-iron bunny add a whimsical touch.

Neubert's talents have been recognized by the community. Her yard was featured on the 2007 Soroptimist Garden Tour. That same year, she was awarded second place for Best Use of Space in a beautification contest sponsored by the city.

The yard continues to have color in all seasons. Pots of chrysanthemums adorn the porch and entry garden in fall. At Christmas, the front yard and the iron fence along the driveway are decorated with baskets of evergreen boughs, pinecones, and ribbons, along with strings of colored lights. In all ways, the garden allows Neubert to celebrate and honor the rituals of life: the people who are important, the seasons that pass, and the cycle of life itself.

Mona Neubert's passion for interior design is also evident in her garden, which is decorated with a pleasing mix of Victorian artifacts.

Not only are curved beds more pleasing to the eye than straight-sided beds, they also make Barbara Glaser's garden feel larger. *Right:* Coleus and chartreuse hostas brighten the entrance to the former church, now used as office space.

Reclaiming a Green Space by Design

For community advocate, educator, and conservationist Barbara Glaser, historic preservation is just one of her many passions. The restoration of School No. 4 on Spring Street was the latest and perhaps most ambitious of the projects undertaken by her firm, Linell Lands. The structure, built in 1911 and designed by noted architect R. Newton Brezee, was used by the city school district until 2003. The classic three-story brick building was remodeled and upgraded and is now home to more than a dozen small businesses, including several nonprofit groups.

One of Glaser's earliest projects was the former Newland Mission Chapel, adjacent to the school, which she purchased in the mid-1970s and converted into commercial space. The church was part of Temple Grove Seminary, owned by Charles F. Dowd, who is best known for initiating modern standardized time zones. The Romanesque-style chapel, built in 1870, was subsequently occupied by several different denominations over the years.

Glaser's enthusiasm for preservation extends to her love of gardening. She later purchased and moved into a house next to the church's parking lot, which had been paved around a grove of majestic white oaks. To save the old trees, Glaser decided to reclaim the green space between the house and the church. The asphalt was removed, exposing earth that was extremely compacted by the pavement and the weight of the cars. The ground was loosened and aerated to allow oxygen and nutrients to penetrate the surface. Loads of compost and other rich amendments were added to correct the soil's acidic pH and allow it to once again support plant life.

While her kids were still young, Glaser's yard was planted with vegetables in raised beds and was also used as a play area. In the late 1990s, after the children were grown, Glaser began converting the beds into ornamental flower borders. In collaboration with landscape architect Cynthia Behan, a design was created to incorporate meandering grass pathways that would connect separate garden rooms made for sitting, eating, and strolling.

The stately oaks were the most striking and significant element of the original yard, and Glaser wanted to include them as an integral part of the design. The high tree canopy provides cool, dappled shade on warm summer days, and the lyrical movement of light breezes through the leaves adds to the ambiance. The existing gardens lacked a basic foundation, causing the visual focus to extend away from the space and into the neighboring homes. Behan's design incorporated small trees, shrubs, perennials, and ground covers of varying heights to create a layered understory.

Arbors, furniture, and prominent plants offer focal points for the eye to rest. The lush footpaths were constructed in gentle curves (rather than straight), making the space feel larger and resulting in more pleasing vignettes. The church, the house, and the "Little House," a former children's playhouse, were also incorporated into the design as a backdrop. Between the playhouse and the chapel is a secluded haven with a wooden arbor and a love-seat swing that looks back onto the garden.

A wooden deck off the house was extended, and an adjoining brick patio was installed to create a spacious sitting area, where Glaser and her husband, Paul Zachos, often enjoy a leisurely dinner or a morning cup of coffee. The patio is edged with a bed of waist-high daylilies, which creates a gentle transition into the rest of the garden. A six-foot wooden fence with two gates encloses the entire yard, allowing for privacy from the busy urban street just a few feet away. The resulting effect is that of a secret sanctuary that instantly transports visitors into a tranquil world apart from the bustle of the city.

Small flowering dogwoods and river birch (*Betula nigra* 'Heritage') are planted at strategic point in the beds and along the pathways, providing the basic structure and focal points that draw the eye through the landscape. The understory is brightened with shade-tolerant perennials with interesting foliage, including speckle-leaved lungwort, chartreuse and powder blue hostas, Siberian bugloss (*Brunnera macrophylla*

'Jack Frost'), and bronze coral bells (*Heuchera*). New cultivars of coral bells developed in recent years come in a dizzying array of foliage colors, including gold, lime green, purple, orange, or red, some with veining, spots, or deep ruffles.

In an island bed that Glaser refers to as the "fairy garden," hostas with wide margins of white, yellow, or lime green offer additional contrast and visual interest. In early summer, clumps of feather flower (*Astilbe simplicifolia* 'Sprite') produce sprays of soft cream-colored plumes. A back corner of the property near the playhouse receives enough light to support Asiatic lilies, coneflower (*Echinacea*), gooseneck loosestrife (*Lysimachia clethroides*), speedwell (*Veronica*), and climbing trumpet vine (*Campsis radicans*).

The yard is a haven for wildlife, and Glaser enjoys watching the birds that congregate at several feeders. Some vistas were created to be enjoyed from inside the house, where Glaser can comfortably view her feathered visitors in winter. The garden is maintained organically with no chemicals or pesticides, to retain a healthy environment for two-legged and winged friends alike.

The beds are replenished each spring with compost made from decomposed matter from the yard. Beneficial nematodes, which are microscopic worms, control a wide array of pests, including Japanese beetles, cutworms, weevils, and grubs. A cocoa bean mulch, with the faint scent of chocolate, helps suppress weeds and reduces the need for supplemental watering.

Other meandering beds incorporate a well-orchestrated tapestry of reliable perennials, including daylilies, ligularia (*L. przewalskii*), boltonia, bleeding heart (*Dicentra spectabilis*), bee balm, plume poppy (*Macleaya microcarpa*), bellflower (*Campanula*), and lady's mantle. The borders are punctuated with an occasional shrub, including viburnum (*V. carlesii* and *V.* x *burkwoodii*), rugosa roses, and hydrangeas. A laceleaf Japanese maple (*Acer palmatum dissectum*) is a focal point enjoyed from the Little House. A storm in recent years felled one of the white oaks, wiping out a swath of plantings along the chapel. Glaser wanted to restore color in this area quickly, so she planted drifts of orange-red coleus (which perfectly match the building's brick facade) combined with contrasting chartreuse hostas.

There are personal touches as well. The most cherished plants have been given by loved ones over the years. The cuttings that survived from Glaser's grandmother, or seeds and divisions given by lifelong friends, elicit fond memories and sentimental feelings. A small gnome figurine, nestled alongside the playhouse, was a gift from Glaser to her husband, Paul, when they first married, symbolizing his new place in the garden and in her life.

Glaser enjoys sharing the space with others and invites the tenants of her adjacent office buildings to spend their lunch hour or breaks there in good weather. The garden was also featured twice on the Soroptimist Garden Tour, including its tenth-anniversary tour showcasing the most popular gardens from past years. This urban sanctuary, which Glaser rescued from layers of asphalt, has in turn rewarded her with a place of personal respite and renewal. ❧

Top: The "Little House" was formerly the children's playhouse. *Bottom left and right:* Hostas of many colors and sizes fill the beds in the oak-shaded property.

A City IN THE *Country*

Adirondack Style in Saratoga

Saratoga Springs is known as "the city in the country" for its seamless transition from urban streets to bucolic rural scenery. Nowhere is this characterization truer than at the home of Ted and Susan Collins, which sits on the border of Saratoga Springs and the town of Greenfield. The seven-acre property, a stone's throw from the Skidmore College athletic fields, is part of the Putnam Creek watershed. Five acres of the seven-acre parcel consist of water: a stream, a pond, and marshes.

When the couple moved here in 1993, they inherited a small flower garden created by the previous owner. Though Susan had never gardened, she decided to tend the plot, located under a small grove of trees near the house. She began perusing books and magazines, and with the help of an old friend she learned how to care for the plants.

Right: The Collinses' flagstone patio merges seamlessly with an alpine rock garden in the right foreground. *Above:* Tall plantings such as Joe-Pye weed and perennial sunflowers define the border beds and provide screening.

Susan found she enjoyed the process of digging in the soil and watching things grow. She began expanding the gardens around the house and into the natural areas in back. Tall stands of golden perennial sunflowers and purple Joe-Pye weed frame the neighboring farm outbuildings. Clumps of black-eyed Susan, phlox, daylilies, and ornamental grasses are integrated with native plants, blurring the distinction between cultivated gardens and wildlife habitat.

Ted and Susan Collins are particularly fond of the Adirondack rustic look, which suits the rural setting of their property. The style, which utilizes natural materials—namely logs and stone—originated with William West Durant, who built the first "Great Camp" in Adirondack Park during the 1870s. A recent addition to their home included an Adirondack-style front porch with post-and-beam construction, a rough-hewn stone facade, and rustic furniture. The entry foundation is softened with simple plantings of hosta, ferns, and daylilies. Another rustic feature on the property is a twig gazebo, which sits along the marsh at the back of a wide swath of mowed grass. The cedar structure was custom made by Romancing the Woods, based in Woodstock, New York (www.romancingthewoods.com). Alongside the house is a rustic flagstone patio edged by alpine and perennial gardens.

A country-style garden shed across the gravel driveway from the home's entrance provides an attractive focal point to a shade garden. The shed, built by a cousin in Massachusetts in the 1990s, was brought to the property by Susan's father. It was painted a soft brown and beige and decorated with a custom stained-glass window.

Susan likes to think of the garden as a blank canvas to be painted with the blooms, textures, and foliage of plants. She strives not for a formal design but to incorporate favorite plants into the landscape. She'll often return from a trip to one of her favorite nurseries—Oligny's Country Gardens, Toadflax Nursery, or Sunnyside Gardens—with a carload of plants and no clear idea of where to put them. She'll walk around the yard, plant in hand, until she spies the perfect place. Many of her shade plants, including hostas, come from Shades of Green in Charlton (ww.lotsahosta.com).

An alpine garden at the edge of the stone patio is a woven tapestry of low-growing plants, including a silvery carpet of woolly thyme (*Thymus pseudolanuginosus*) and a collection of succulent sedums and sempervivums. One of the more unusual specimens is a prickly pear cactus (*Opuntia*) from a friend in Rochester; Collins hopes that this USDA Zone 4 plant will survive. Three varieties of grape—'Marquis', 'Reliance', and Concord—thrive in the sheltered microclimate next to the patio.

Ted and Susan take pride in using local materials and labor to renovate their home and landscape. The quartzite flagstone used for the patio is from a quarry in Whitehall; other gravel and stones were mined from two quarries just up the road from their home. Timbers used in their Adirondack-style addition came from Kingsbury. Ted worked alongside

Above: A lovely garden shed is the focal point of a shade border at the edge of the gravel drive. The large-leaved hosta at far right is 'Sum and Substance'.
Upper right: The Adirondack-style porch with rough-hewn rock facade is a recent addition to the house. *Right:* A layered mixed border near the house was already well established when the Collinses moved here in 1993.

Chris Gregory of CG Stone of Saratoga Springs to locate the stone and build the patio.

Because their property borders a protected watershed and wildlife habitat, Ted and Susan garden organically, shunning any chemical pesticides or herbicides. Susan's secret weapon to growing healthy plants is what she jokingly refers to as her "million-dollar horse poop." Each year, she orders six to ten yards of aged horse manure from a local mulch company. The soil amendment, which comes from area stables, is spread in a generous layer over all the flower beds in spring. Most animal waste, especially from horses, is best if allowed to sit for a season. It then has time to break down into rich compost, the heat of the decomposition killing weed seeds and pathogens. Any minor insect damage or disease that shows up on garden plants is taken in stride, considered part of nature's course. The goal is not perfection but a coexistence with nature.

A hair stylist by trade, Susan has a salon adjacent to the Alpine Sport Shop. A small outbuilding was converted into the salon, which she decorates with potted plants, hanging baskets, and perennials. The unfinished-log entrance and Adirondack loveseat add a rustic touch. The neighborly rapport that Ted and Susan Collins have established with Cathy and Jack Hay, the sports shop's owners, extends to the garden as well. Ted and Susan's property was featured twice on the annual Soroptimist Garden Tour, including the "best of" tenth-anniversary tour.

A Love of the Outdoors

For Cathy Hay, gardening is just a part of the life that she and her husband, Jack, have made for themselves on their country property just outside of town. The flowers and beds are an extension of their love of nature and the outdoor living areas created from Jack's penchant for building things.

Cathy's parents owned the Alpine Sport Shop, which was originally part of the old Skidmore College campus near the center of town. The store, located on Spring Street, sold women's clothing as well as sporting goods. When the new campus was built, the business moved as well. A new store was built in 1968 at its present location on Clinton Street near Skidmore's athletic fields.

Jack and Cathy, high school sweethearts who met on their school's ski team, married in 1971 and moved into a mobile home on two acres behind the store. Ten years later, they built the Swiss chalet–style home they now live in, and eventually took over management of the ski shop. Jack built much of the house himself, installing passive solar heat, a relatively new technology at the time. He also constructed a potting shed for Cathy from wood recycled from his mother's crumbling carriage house on Circular Street. The quaint lean-to–style shed, complete with storage shelves, counter space, and an antique sink, was the perfect place for Cathy to spend time with her plants. The shed was decorated over the years with antique watering cans, an Adirondack-style chandelier, old wooden skis, and other whimsical knick-knacks. Cathy painted a mural on the inside of the door and added a custom stained-glass window and lacy curtains.

Top left and bottom right: Cathy Hay's garden shed is full of whimsy and personal touches. *Bottom left and top right:* A twig-style bench and a pair of Adirondack chairs invite visitors to pause and enjoy the restful setting.

One of Cathy's first gardens was a long perennial border alongside the fence that encircles an inground swimming pool adjacent to the house. She planted reliable North Country perennials, including daylilies, tickseed, bee balm, baby's breath *(Gypsophila)*, Shasta daisies, coneflower, astilbes, and perennial sunflowers. In the lawn between the fence and potting shed is a small oval bed of aromatic lavender *(Lavandula angustifolia* 'Hidcote') and a sundial as the centerpiece. Next to the potting shed, which is more shaded, are specimens of large-leaved hostas, daylilies, and ferns. The shed's exterior is adorned with window boxes and other homey touches.

In the late 1980s, the Hays built an outdoor playhouse for their two children. The tiny one-room cabin, decorated with green shutters, white curtains, and petunia-filled flower boxes, is now enjoyed by their young grandson. A spring-fed swamp nearby was dredged by a nephew and converted into a bucolic pond, where the family enjoys sitting on the several rustic benches placed around the water's edge. The pond, its banks softened by native and aquatic plants, is home to dozens of frogs, their occasional croaking a charming sound on warm summer days. Jack's most ambitious building project (other than their home) was an adult-

size tree house, a two-year project completed in 2004. The rustic cabin on stilts overlooks the pond and is accessible by a wooden staircase. The structure includes a small screened-in porch, a comfortably furnished bedroom, and a library/reading area. The tree house is even equipped with modern conveniences: electric lights, a miniature refrigerator, and a working bathroom; an outdoor shower is underneath. The treetop haven, even though just steps from their home, gives the Hays a sense of their own personal getaway in the woods. They spend many nights here in summer and use it as a seasonal guesthouse for visitors. A flower border along the front consists of an informal mix of daylilies, ferns, hostas, hydrangeas, and lungwort, which complement the wooded setting.

Along with the salvaged carriage house materials used for the potting shed, there are other sentimental touches around the property. An old-fashioned rose growing on an arbor came from the garden of Cathy's grandmother, who once lived on North Street. Log planters at the entrance to the house were made by the Hays' son-in-law. Antique skis that adorn the inside of the potting shed were given by customers of the sports shop. Cathy still nurtures her first garden, a small hidden sanctuary that overlooks the property.

The Hays' next-door neighbor, Susan Collins, is also an avid gardener. Even though their gardens are somewhat different in style, the neighboring gardeners have enjoyed a long friendship that includes the exchange of lots of gardening tips.

A Personal Sanctuary

Martha Rossi and her husband, Michael, always dreamed of having their own home, and their wish came true when they purchased a modest brick house on the outskirts of Saratoga Springs. They expanded their new home with an addition in 2003 and completed an outdoor deck and gazebo in 2004. When Martha's sister commented that the post-construction mess looked depressing, Martha knew she had to do something. The small backyard, which backs up to a wooded area, attracted a charming assortment of wildlife, but it lacked character.

Martha enlisted the help of Dick Thayer of Saratoga Landscape Company and Susie Kane-Kettlewell of Garden Masters to create a private space for personal renewal, a place where Martha could unwind from the demands of her job. The team arrived at a design that was both functional and aesthetic and made the best use of the small wedged-shaped lot, using curved beds to give the garden a sense of movement and make the entire space flow effortlessly together.

In the sunny area at the front of the house, mixed borders surround a swatch of lawn. Though the space is tiny, it contains an impressive array of structural plants. Small and medium-size trees include magnolia, weeping cherry (*Prunus* 'Pendula'), Japanese maple (*Acer palmatum*), and weeping Alaskan cedar (*Chamaecyparis nootkatensis* 'Pendula'). A diverse tapestry of shrubs consists of boxwood, spirea, barberry, lilac (*Syringa vulgaris*), and roses. Ornamental grasses include blue oat grass (*Helictotrichon sempervirens*), maiden grass, and fescue (*Festuca*).

The "bones" of the mixed border are filled in with sturdy perennials—bee balm, coneflower, black-eyed Susan, iris, daylilies, phlox, foxgloves (*Digitalis*), and sedums. Annual vinca, Million Bells, lantana, and wishbone flower (*Torenia*) are planted in gaps along the front for summerlong color. For more visual impact, plants are grouped to create large drifts of color.

A Rose of Sharon (*Hibiscus syriacus*) planted near the house foundation came from a local farmers' market. It's situated in a warm microclimate, south-facing, sheltered from wind, and receiving lots of reflected warmth from the brick facade. (An identical specimen sited out near the curb died after its first year.) A heavy mulch in fall gives additional protection. The rose mallow grows several feet taller than its stated maximum height of eight feet, and is covered with saucer-size pink blooms in August and September.

At the entrance to the back garden is a romantic white lattice arbor flanked by two tree hydrangeas (*H. paniculata* 'Grandiflora') and a hedge of burning bush (*Euonymus alatus*), which turns brilliant red in fall. Rough-hewn stepping stones seem to float in a river of golden creeping Jenny. Because much of the back garden is in shade at least part of the day, variegated plants, including striped hostas, Siberian bugloss, Japanese painted fern, and Jacob's ladder (*Polemonium caeruleum* 'Brise D'Anjou') were used to brighten up the space.

A lush green lawn rimmed with flowers leads to several separate garden areas. The lines of a screened gazebo at the edge of a wooden deck are softened with late-summer color from coneflower, black-eyed Susan, and maiden grass. A semicircular graveled area surrounded by pots of brightly colored annuals is home to two Adirondack-style loungers. One of Martha's favorite areas is the adjacent water feature: a gentle waterfall and a small round pond surrounded by golden Japanese sweetflag *(Acorus gramineus)* and pale pink rosebud impatiens. In a small corner is a hidden sanctuary with a statue of Saint Francis and a stone bench shaded by a spring-blooming lilac *(Syringa vulgaris)*.

Moles and voles are a recurring problem as they burrow underground and eat the bulbs of some plants. Martha grows her canna lilies and elephant's ear in black plastic pots sunk into the ground to deter the pests. Deer still visit the yard, but for the most part they stay on a trail near the edge of the property and don't ravage the garden. The Rossis maintain a peaceful coexistence with their wild visitors.

The Rossis spend a great deal of time in their yard, whether it's to cook leisurely dinner on the grill or to sit on the deck and listen to the water sounds on a warm evening. Like their dream of owning their own home, the goal of having an outdoor sanctuary has also come to a satisfying conclusion.

Far left: Late-summer–blooming perennials flank the screened gazebo on the Rossis' deck. *Center:* Pale pink rosebud impatiens and green-gold Japanese sweetflag brighten the edges of a small waterfall and pool. Golden creeping Jenny carpets the stepping stones leading to the back garden. *Right:* The spectacular hibiscus in the small front garden came from a local farmers' market.

A Decorator's Eye

When Mark Hogan moved into his Saratoga residence in 1994, the house's interior needed a personal touch, and the yard comprised just a few plants and a poorly seeded lawn. When Rob Saba moved into the house in 1998, the two renovated the home to reflect what they call a "Ralph Lauren country-casual" taste. They then focused on the outside, gradually transforming it over the next ten years.

They installed a healthy new lawn along with a diverse mix of trees, shrubs, and perennials. Crimson Japanese barberries *(Berberis thunbergii)*, gold-leaved Japanese spirea *(S. japonica)*, cotoneaster, and burning bush provide structure to perennial borders of daylilies, fall-blooming sedums, and reliable black-eyed Susan. A border planting of *Rosa* 'The Fairy', a hardy antique shrub rose with cascading waves of pink-blushed blooms, flowers all summer long. Metallic blue Colorado spruce *(Picea pungens glauca)*, white fir *(Abies concolor)*, and other evergreens of varying shapes and height round out the landscape with year-round color.

Hogan, a vice president for Saratoga National Bank & Trust Company, and Saba, who does fund-raising for the Albany Medical Center, enjoy weekend getaways to out-of-the-way places. On one of their trips, they became enamored with a lattice pergola shelter and persuaded local artisans Steve Coulombe and Tim Stockman to build them something similar.

The lattice-sided pergola Hogan designed became the framework for an outdoor living room. Earth-tone curtains, an area rug, and a wrought-iron chandelier provide elegant touches, complementing the casual patio seating. Climbing vines and shrubs soften the lines of the arbor, while ferns and houseplants provide living accents. The floor of local slate and finely crushed pea gravel is easily cleaned with the quick spray of a hose.

Next, Hogan and Saba constructed a low wall of river rock along the tree line similar to those found on nearby farmsteads. The remaining yard was enclosed with a custom-built fence made by Bill Pogonowski of Adirondack Fence.

In 2003, Michael Phinney, of Phinney Design Group (www.phinneydesign.com), helped them draw up plans for a two-room year-round porch off the back of the house. The glass-enclosed porch contains a rustic stone fireplace and casual seating and is a cozy place to sip coffee or a glass of wine with friends. Flagstone steps connect to the slate patio, another casual outdoor room, adorned with a wicker couch

Far right and top: Beautifully landscaped beds and an abundance of container plantings invite visitors to linger in the welcoming outdoor rooms at the Hogan-Saba house. *Right:* Pink, magenta, and deep purple were the colors chosen for this summer bed of cosmos and other annuals.

and chair, glass coffee table, throw rugs, and other decorative accents. Making good use of their inviting outdoor rooms, Hogan and Saba delight in hosting yard parties for friends and neighbors.

Each year, Hogan and Saba add new plants, try different plant combinations, and rotate flowers and accessories to reflect the seasons. The process starts in April, when they visit nearby Sunnyside Gardens to order annual flowers for summer. Sunnyside's owner Ned Chapman utilizes an artist's color wheel to help them select compatible hues. To complement their house's soft beige exterior. A typical planting might include dwarf pink 'Sonata' cosmos, blue 'Wave' petunias, yellow tickseed, purple verbena, purple fairy fan-flower, pink Million Bells, and gold licorice plant *(Helichrysum petiolare)*. Along the front porch, hanging baskets and black Victorian urns burst with splashes of color.

Fall is their favorite season. The summer annuals are replaced with chrysanthemums in autumnal tones of orange, gold, burgundy, rust, and yellow, and the yard is decorated with a showy display of cornstalks, pumpkins, squash, gourds, dried flower arrangements, and pinecones.

In winter, pine boughs and wreaths are hung in most of the windows. Saba makes the evergreen garland ropes to drape around the fences, front porch, and light posts. Thousands of tiny lights cast a gentle glow after dusk, drawing neighbors and far-flung visitors to view the festive display.

With demanding full-time jobs and three teenage boys, finding time to maintain the attractive landscape is a challenge. "The key is to do a little bit each day," says Saba. The two spend an hour or so most days after work watering and deadheading the flowers, which encourages new blooms. It's also a time to unwind from their long, hectic workdays. On weekends, they devote an additional two to three hours weeding, pruning, and grooming. The lawn is mowed twice a week. Every ten days, the annuals are fed with a dose of Miracle-Gro Bloom Booster to keep color coming all season long.

Now ready for a new challenge, Saba and Hogan are building a new house closer to town, where they look forward to being able to walk to nearby restaurants and shops. They eagerly anticipate starting over with a new yard that will be smaller and easier to care for. For them, the process is as much fun as the end result. ❧

Above: The front yard is lavishly decorated for fall. *Right:* A lattice pergola frames an elegant outdoor living room.

Out-of-Town Landscapes

A Garden for the Winner's Circle

Part of Saratoga's summertime culture is the influx of horse trainers, jockeys, owners, and track personnel who participate in the six-week thoroughbred meet. Since the first event at Horse Haven in 1863, some of the biggest names in racing have come to try their hand at winning: trainers Wayne Lukas, Nick Zito, and Barclay Tagg; jockeys Jerry Bailey, Angel Cordero, and John Valazquez; and the owners and breeders responsible for the horses. Many of these seasonal residents own their own homes, ranging from modest ranch abodes near the track to some of the city's grandest mansions and sprawling estates outside of town.

One of these part-time residents, Malvern Burroughs, was an unlikely hero to harness racing. In a tale reminiscent of the legendary Seabiscuit, Burroughs and his stallion Malabar Man seemed like dubious entrants to racing. The three-year-old horse had suffered illness and injury, and Burroughs, the standardbred's owner and breeder, was battling his own life-threatening health issues. Yet in 1997, Burroughs would steer Malabar Man to victory in one of harness racing's most illustrious events, The Hambletonian. Burroughs is one of just two amateur drivers in history to accomplish this feat. Malabar Man also finished first in the Breeder's Crown, guided by Burroughs, the first amateur driver to win the stakes race. During his

Colorful flower beds and lawn jockeys painted in their stable's colors mark
the entrance to the Burroughs estate. *Inset:* A hedge of hydrangeas fronted by
magenta astilbe makes a dramatic sight in July.

career, Malabar Man won other top races, including the Toyota Bluegrass Stakes, the World Trotting Derby, and the Orsi Mangelli in Milan, Italy. Upon retirement, the stallion would go on to sire a long list of successful foals with combined winnings of more than $25 million. In 2008, Malabar Man was inducted into the Living Horse Hall of Fame at the Harness Racing Museum in Goshen, New York.

Today, Burroughs and his wife, Janet, make Saratoga their summer home. They remain active in the equine world, with part or full ownership in dozens of horses on farms around the East Coast. In the fall of 2004, they moved to their sprawling estate north of Saratoga Lake, a two-year-old home with an unfinished landscape of bare rocks and topsoil.

With the help of Darryl and Leslie's Design (now Cedar Tree Muse, www.cedartree.com), they built a multilevel tiered landscape in back with a series of stone patios, a porch gazebo, an inground swimming pool with a waterfall, and an authentic bocce ball court. A local pool builder installed the kidney-shaped inground pool and plumbed the waterfall. The screened-in gazebo, where Malvern and Janet often enjoy a leisurely meal or beverages, overlooks the pool to one side and a spectacular view of the valley below. In front, a stone staircase and adjacent stone berms provide the framework for extensive plantings of shrubs, trees, and perennials. Much of the hardscaping is from local sources, including Heldeberg bluestone, Adirondack granite from Fort Ann, and tan quartzite from Whitehall. Pavers used for the sidewalks and around the pool were installed in a European-style method that incorporates interlocking concrete pieces.

Malvern and Janet worked closely with Dick Thayer of Saratoga Landscape Company to select trees and shrubs that have multiseason interest and are easy to care for. Susie Kane-Kettlewell of Garden Masters lent her expertise in perennials. Annuals, which provide summerlong color, are provided by Sunnyside Gardens and are installed by a few of their employees who do landscape work on the side.

Two beds flanking the driveway entrance are planted in perfect mirror images. Perennial 'Stella de Oro' daylilies, bee balm, maiden grass, sedums, tickseed, and ferns are interplanted with colorful annual 'Sonata' cosmos, yellow marigolds, ageratum, dusty miller, and plumed cockscomb. The long, winding driveway is flanked with honeylocust (*Gleditsia triacanthos*), which are encircled with miniature flower gardens. Flowering plums produce snow-white blooms in early spring, followed by deep burgundy leaves throughout the summer. A raised stone garden where the driveway circles around has a life-size metal horse statue as its centerpiece. The dramatic equine with flowing mane and tail seems to float above a sea of burgundy verbena, purple petunias, and bright orange-red daylilies.

The entry garden is a mixed border of trees, shrubs, and perennials set amongst the stone hardscaping. 'Green Mountain' hybrid boxwood (*Buxus* 'Green Mountain', a cross

Above: A sloping rock garden and carefully placed plantings soften the perimeter of the swimming pool. *Right:* Semicircular stone stairs lead from the pool to the house.

of *B. sempervirens* and *B. microphylla* var. *koreana*) line the sidewalk, and to the left of the entry is a Japanese flowering dogwood (*Cornus kousa*), which has multiseason interest: showy pagoda-shape flowers in late spring, red berries in summer, and scarlet foliage in fall. 'Bloodgood' Japanese maples (*Acer palmatum atropurpureum* 'Bloodgood') and laceleaf Japanese maples contrast with the powder blue foliage of Wichita Blue juniper (*Juniperus scopulorum* 'Wichita Blue').

At the western edge of the expansive front lawn is a dramatic display of mophead hydrangeas and 150 specimens of astilbe (*A. chinensis* 'Visions') planted in an S configuration that conforms to the natural tree line. The showy 'Visions' series of astilbes is more drought tolerant than many other varieties, and is also deer resistant. On the east side of the house, mounding 'Crimson Pygmy' barberries (*Berberis thunbergii* 'Crimson Pigmy') contrast perfectly with a backdrop of columnar-shaped evergreens. Long-blooming, low-maintenance perennials such as Shasta daisy, black-eyed Susan, tickseed, and gayfeather planted among the shrubs offer weeks of color.

In the backyard, small island beds built in at the edge of the pool are planted with bright red annual geraniums, annual periwinkle (*Catharanthus*), and purple fountain grass. A rock garden reminiscent of a mountain alpine meadow overlooks the pool. The stone facade with pockets of rich soil is planted with annuals selected by Malvern Burroughs, who prefers lots of bright color. Purple petunias, yellow marigolds, dwarf pink cosmos, and portulaca in tropical hues of hot pink and orange spill down the bank. The top of the stone berm is planted with Knock Out roses and clumps of pink and yellow coneflower for extra height. Knock Out rose, a newer variety, is a reliable and sturdy choice for North Country gardens, needing little maintenance and blooming for most of the season. Golden creeping Jenny and other perennial ground covers soften the craggy boulders.

Malvern and Janet's richly decorated property, a collaborative effort by some of Saratoga's most talented landscapers, stonemasons, and gardeners, has resulted in a landscape worthy of being in any winner's circle.

A Teaching Garden

It's said that our lives are shaped by the roads we choose to go down. For Kerry Ann Mendez, this happened in the most literal sense, on the road she took to work each day. The daily commute to her job as admissions counselor at Union College took her past Smalltown Perennials (now closed) in Burnt Hills. As Mendez drove by the colorful displays of eye-catching flowers, she daydreamed of a job that would bring her outdoors.

On a whim, Mendez stopped at the nursery one day to inquire about a part-time job. Though she had no experience with plants, her enthusiasm won over the owner, Melba Higgins. Mendez was hired to work two days a week during the growing season, where she learned about plants from the ground up. She took to the job like a duck to water, working at the nursery part-time for eight years while keeping her position at Union College.

With the encouragement of friends and family, Mendez started her own plant-related business. She left the security of her full-time academia job in 2003 and began teaching garden workshops at her home in Ballston Spa. Working at home allows her more time with her son, Evan, and husband, Sergio. Her gardens became an outdoor classroom as she offered eager students a hands-on opportunity to get their hands dirty. She taught basic design concepts, soil preparation, and garden maintenance. And her students ate it all up.

As word spread, Mendez was invited to speak at local garden clubs and flower shows. She began writing gardening articles for local newspapers, as well as regional and national magazines such as *Fine Gardening*. Her energy and love of plants were contagious, and she developed a local following.

Since starting her business, which she named Perennially Yours, Mendez has taught more than seven thousand students. Her open gardens, held once a month from May to August, draw up to two hundred visitors at a time. Mendez's website, where she publishes an online newsletter, draws six thousand hits a month. She offers design and consulting services and speaks to groups from Virginia to Maine. Many Saratoga-area gardeners mention Mendez as an inspiration for their own gardens.

In 2004, Mendez founded the annual Great Gardens and Landscaping Symposium, held in spring at the landmark Mirror Lake Inn in Lake Placid, among other locations. The two-day event typically draws a hundred to two hundred attendees and an impressive array of regional and national sponsors. Several speakers host workshops, roundtable discussions, and book signings, and there is casual time for socializing.

Mendez's approach to gardening is to keep things simple and as low maintenance as possible. She emphasizes building healthy soil as the crucial foundation to a bountiful garden. Plants grown in rich soil are healthier and stronger, making them more resistant to pests and diseases. Sturdy, reliable plants that naturally need little fuss are the basis for her own gardens and those she designs. Her approach emphasizes organic practices that utilize few or no chemicals or pesticides.

The soil in Mendez's one-quarter-acre garden is heavy clay, which poses a drainage challenge. She brought in yards of horse manure and cow manure mixed with sand (to aid with drainage), and also utilized compost made from leaves and grass clippings. She occasionally purchases compost made by the Saratoga Springs department of public works at their facility on Waibel Avenue. She mixes the amendments eight to twelve inches deep into the soil, then allows the raised beds to settle before planting. After the plants are installed, another layer of compost is added to serve as a mulch.

In spring, Mendez broadcasts a slow-release 5-5-5 organic fertilizer on the beds just as the plants are breaking dormancy. She gives an extra boost to lily bulbs, clematis, roses, and astilbes with a dose of Plant-tone, an all-purpose organic plant food. The results are breathtaking; by summer, the borders are lush with foliage and flowers, and the lilies (whose bulbs reach softball size) tower an impressive eight feet above the surrounding landscape.

Mendez's favorite plants are like old friends; they never let her down and are reliable year after year. In addition to the old standbys of hostas and daylilies, Mendez favors coral bells for their range of foliage texture and color; the cranesbill geranium hybrid 'Rozeanne', which blooms from June to October; and masterwort (Astrantia), which tolerates a wide variety of soil and light conditions. For roses, she prefers the sturdy Knock Out series, including the double red and pink varieties, and climbers 'New Dawn' and 'Fourth of July'. One of the most reliable roses is 'William Baffin', a Canadian Explorer shrub rose hardy to USDA Zone 3 that can also be trained as a climber.

With varying conditions around her yard, siting plants in the proper place is crucial. In the far back, under towering deciduous trees, is a large shade garden with a patchwork of hostas of all colors and variegations, combined with astilbe, bishop's hat, primrose (Primula), nettle, coral bells, and lady's mantle. Most of these plants tolerate a wide variety of light and soil conditions. In a quiet corner, a small pond with the soothing sound of trickling water is surrounded by brightly colored foliage plants. Along both sides of the long, narrow lot are boisterous sun borders brimming with dozens of perennials that bloom at various times throughout the season. With the wide diversity of areas in her yard, and the success she's had with them, the space is a living example of the importance of caring for plants properly.

Mendez works with local and national growers to trial new varieties to see what will do best in her garden. The feedback that growers get from gardeners all over the country helps them recommend the best plants for different regions. It also assists Mendez in advising her students. Her enthusiastic style and passion for plants has helped gardeners in Saratoga and beyond to succeed and experience new joy in their own yards. She hopes her students will find, as she has for herself, that tending the earth takes the focus off daily problems and feeds the soul.

Kerry Ann Mendez's shade garden is a study in rich texture and color.

A Masterful Landscape

Like many gardeners, Sandy and Jim Wimet started out small, with just a single bed alongside their home. "We grew vegetables, but not much else," Sandy recalls. When she discovered ornamental perennials, Sandy began digging out an area along a tall wooden fence on the west side of the property and developed a perennial flower border.

After thirty-five years of living in their Middle Grove home and raising their children, the Wimets began to devote more time to their country homestead. Sandy, a former clerk for the board of elections, and Jim, who worked for the state social services division, are retired. With more time on their hands, they were able to develop gardens throughout the property that serve specific functions: a cutting garden, a kitchen garden (including a vast array of herbs and vegetables), a sunny perennial border, an ornamental shade garden, and a fenced water garden.

The country acreage was once an active farm, so the soil contains more loam than sand. The beds are regularly amended with compost made from grass clippings, leaves, kitchen scraps, horse manure, and trimmings from nondiseased garden plants. In spring, an all-purpose 5-10-5 granular fertilizer is broadcast on all the beds. New perennials receive a dose of bonemeal mixed into the planting hole. Annuals are treated to a regular dose of Miracle-Gro liquid fertilizer, which provides a quick burst of nutrients.

The floral display begins in April, when snowdrops and crocus push their way up through the late-winter snow. Other early bloomers soon follow, including daffodils, glory-of-the-snow *(Chionodoxa)*, squill *(Scilla)*, and trillium, one of Sandy's favorite plants.

For Sandy, a Master Gardener with the Saratoga County Cornell Cooperative Extension, horticulture goes beyond tending the family homestead. She was certified as a Master Gardener in 2002 and participates in ongoing training sessions once a month. She also participates in a horticulture therapy group, teaching floral arranging and indoor garden techniques at area nursing homes.

Detailed record keeping helps Sandy keep track of the plants in her own garden, including how well they perform. She maintains a thorough accounting of each perennial, including the botanical name; where it is planted; its height, color, and bloom time; where it was purchased; and the price. She keeps a separate journal, where she notes the daily weather conditions and what's flowering that week. During peak bloom season in July and August, the latter entry can be quite long.

Island beds flourish beneath mature pines in the Wimets' backyard. *Inset:* Bugleweed *(Ajuga* 'Burgundy glow') carpets the ground at the edge of the shade garden.

Sandy finds it difficult to name a particular plant as her favorite. "I like whatever is blooming at the time," she says. A sentimental favorite is bread-seed poppies, whose seed she saves each year and re-scatters in spring. The original seeds, a gift from her grandmother, date to the 1970s. As a youngster, involvement in 4-H and helping out in her grandmother's garden gave Sandy an early foundation for her love of plants.

Other favorites include the modern hybrid 'Profusion' zinnias, which grow low and bushy, making them an excellent choice for wide swaths of color. They are also known for their exceptionally long bloom time and mildew resistance. Jim especially likes Salvia 'Red Hot Sally', an annual that the Wimets plant in a row along the driveway each spring after the danger of frost is past.

A long perennial border, with peak color in July, grows alongside the busy country road in front. The gaily colored flowers, including daylilies, perennial sunflowers, phlox, mallow *(Malva)*, gayfeather, blue delphiniums, and yarrow *(Achillea)*, are spectacular enough to stop traffic. "People pull into the driveway and jump out of their car to take photos," Sandy says.

The path leading to the house is edged with alternating plants of 'Stella d' Oro' daylilies, 'Profusion Orange' zinnias, and mounds of blue ageratum. A perennial border between the front porch and the garage is an eclectic mix of hosta, astilbe, cranesbill geraniums, bee balm, and tiger lilies *(Lilium lancifolium)*. Next to the front porch is a small water feature, where the Wimets can sit and relax to the soothing sound of trickling water.

Shade borders along the side of the house and in back are home to a rich palette of hostas and other shade lovers. Sandy places contrasting colors and variegations next to each other to help each individual specimen stand out more. The shade borders in back are round island beds planted underneath groves of pine trees.

The original perennial border along the back fence was expanded and is now a brilliant sea of color in summer. Sandy likes the almost discordant combination of scarlet bee balm, orange tiger lilies, hot pink phlox, and yellow sunflowers. A birdbath, and antiques in the beds and hung on the fence, provide interesting focal points.

In 1993, after their kids were grown, the Wimets decided to remove an aboveground swimming pool off the back deck. They took down the outer structure and recycled the lining, using it to construct an inground water garden on the same site. In 2006, the old liner gave out, so the water garden was renovated. The pond was reshaped and a new liner installed, and a waterfall and lighting were added. The picket fence around the former pool is now a rustic backdrop to reliable sun-loving perennials. A row of tall ornamental grasses, planted along the edge of the deck, softens the house foundation and produces color in fall. Hardy cattails, variegated sweet flag, water lilies, and arrowhead thrive in the pond. Nonhardy umbrella plants and elephant's ear are removed and stored indoors over the winter.

The Wimets' country haven is a good illustration of having different areas for separate

The Wimets' sun border is a riot of color in midsummer. *Right:* Black-eyed Susan and zinnias flank the arbor leading to the vegetable garden.

functions, and for siting plants in the right place. It is also beautifully maintained by an agreed-upon division of labor. Jim and Sandy both enjoy certain aspects of the gardens: Sandy does the weeding and design, and Jim does the heavier work of digging holes, moving mulch, and mowing the vast lawn. One of Sandy's favorite tools is her long-handled stirrup hoe, which makes quick work of smaller weeds. The garden offers the Wimets many benefits: it gives them a focus and a shared passion and keeps them active during the growing season. The resulting beautiful flowers are just the icing on the cake.

The Collector's Garden

When Jim and Meg Dalton began gardening at their home in Cohoes, a suburb of Albany, they never imagined they'd run out of room. Shortly after they married in 1987, Jim, a chemical engineer for New York State, and Meg, who worked in academic affairs at Union College, began pursuing their mutual interest in gardening. They dug out swaths of lawn and replaced it with ornamental perennials. A friend told them about Helderledge (www.helderledge.com), a specialty nursery located west of Albany in the village of Altamont. Jim caught his first glimpse of a spectacular eight-foot-wide specimen of a 'Frances Williams' hosta growing at the nursery, and he was hooked. "I'd seen hostas elsewhere, but nothing compared to that," he said.

The Daltons filled their suburban yard with hostas of all sizes and colors, and began collecting other plants to offer some contrast. "It was becoming too monotonous to look at nothing but hostas," Meg recalls. In 1999, they began searching for a larger property, and found the ideal spot in Middle Grove, outside Saratoga Springs. The undeveloped five-acre plot included a quaint Colonial-style house that was painted in colors of brick red and forest green, blending beautifully into the wooded country setting.

More than a hundred trees were removed and the understory was cleared to create a dappled shade garden. The biggest challenge was the soil, which was sandy and largely sterile. The Daltons mulched huge piles of leaves and supplemented the resulting compost with well-rotted horse manure. The first beds, built around the house, were gradually expanded into the surrounding forest. The outer edges were marked off with string, which was moved farther into the woods each year. To keep from being overwhelmed with too much garden, they eventually placed heavy logs around the perimeter to establish a permanent boundary. A neighbor jokingly refers to their log-enclosed plot as "Fort Ticonderoga," in reference to the wooden fortress at the southern end of Lake Champlain.

Two acres of gardens are planted with artful combinations of hostas interspersed with rare and unusual plants collected from nurseries and mail-order sources around the country. Getting plants to bloom in the low-light situation is a challenge. The Daltons

Left to right: The waterfall and pool beside the Dalton house are home to dozens of frogs. The Asian-style horse sculpture and simple cabin demonstrate the Daltons' eclectic tastes. The front entry garden.

rely on shade-tolerant varieties with interesting foliage texture, shape, and color. Plants such as wild ginger, bloodroot (Sanguinaria), and yellow wax bells (Kirengeshoma) are grown primarily for their foliage, although some have the added bonus of attractive flowers. Many plants of Asian origin perform especially well and are suited to the couple's personal style, which they describe as a mix of Asian, Saratogian, and country casual.

The gardens flow along pathways that wind through a canopy of maple, oak, pine, and hemlock. It's hard to tell where the forest ends and the gardens begin. The effect is a seamless blending of unbridled nature and cultivated beds. Several small ponds and a waterfall attract dozens of frogs from the surrounding woods. The sound of moving water, in combination with the croaking frog songs, is at once soothing and hypnotic.

Even though the gardens are sprawling, the Daltons are discerning about the plants they collect. They peruse catalogs from mail-order sources around the country and stop at nurseries whenever they travel. Many specimens found in the garden are unique to the area. Their garden is filled with lesser known plants with alien-sounding names ranging from *Anemonopsis* and *Deinanthe* to *Peltoboykinia*. The Daltons' penchant for the unusual is not for the faint of heart, but this unassuming and generous couple enjoy sharing their enthusiasm for growing and hybridizing, giving freely of their knowledge (and occasionally a division from a treasured specimen).

One of the Daltons' favorite sources for unusual plants is Asiatica Nursery (www .asiaticnursery.com) in Pennsylvania. They also enjoy trying new plants from Seneca

The woodsy garden offers richly landscaped spots to enjoy the view or just visit with friends.

Hill Perennials (www.senecahillperennials.com) and Plant Delights (www.plantdelights .com) in North Carolina. Each of the nurseries offers something different, though all share the same theme of rare plants from around the globe.

A favorite of theirs is hydrangea, particularly the mopheads and lacecaps (*H. macrophylla*), which can be marginal this far north. The Daltons have had good luck with newer varieties developed for colder climates such as 'Endless Summer', which blooms on both old and new wood. Older cultivars, which often die to the ground in harsh winters, usually bloom only on the previous year's growth. Sturdier varieties such as 'Peegee' are reliably hardy and bloom over a long period in late summer and fall. Other favorites include species peonies and double-flowered trilliums.

The Daltons' interest in hostas gradually expanded to hybridizing. The act of crossing plants that possessed their favorite traits to see what would result became a passion. Several beds are devoted solely to propagating and developing new varieties. Hostas, which are grown primarily for their foliage, perform exceptionally well in northern climates. They range in size from several inches across to eight or more feet in diameter, in gold, blue, chartreuse, and every shade of green. Leaves can be deeply variegated, puckered, and shaped like narrow bands or wide hearts. The Daltons concentrate on developing hybrids with their favorite characteristics: solid colors of green or blue, wavy leaf texture, upright structure, leaves with white undersides, and long, arching leaves.

Even though hostas are reliable in northern climates, they do best with some basic care. They prefer regular water and consistently moist soil. A feeding of granular fertilizer (all-purpose 10-10-10 or 20-20-20) ensures optimum growth and overall health. Though they are a shade plant, they do prefer some sun; for a few varieties, coloring is best with morning sun. Too much sun can burn the leaves or alter the color.

Gardening is much more to the Daltons than a mere hobby; they consider it a lifestyle. During the growing season, they are often in the garden from dawn until dusk. They belong to the regional hosta chapter and the American Hosta Society, having attended the national conference each year except one since 2003. They've made a lot of friends along the way, and relish sharing their garden with others. Their garden was one of the most popular on the 2007 Soroptimist Garden Tour.

As much as the Daltons enjoy the rare and unusual, they don't coddle their plants. Because they have such a large garden, varieties have to be able to survive northern winters on their own. Fortunately for them, their favorites also happen to be sturdy—a trait that serves them well. ⚜

Top to bottom: Baby blue flowers and a somewhat sprawling habit distinguish *Clematis heracleifolia* 'Wyevale'. 'Saratoga Sunrise' is one of the Daltons' hybrid hostas. This false anemone—*Anemonopsis macrophylla*—produces striking pale lavender flowers in late summer.

Acknowledgments

Words cannot adequately convey my thanks to all who helped along the journey of creating this book. It simply would not have been possible without the generous and enthusiastic assistance of so many people.

Special thanks go to John Viehman, publisher, and Karin Womer, senior editor, Down East Books, for the opportunity to produce this book, and to Barbara Feller-Roth for copy editing and Lynda Chilton for graphic design.

I am grateful to all of the gardeners who graciously shared their personal spaces and time. I regret I was not able to include them all. Special thanks to: Malvern and Janet Burroughs; Charles and Candace Wait, Barbara Glaser Michele Riggi, Peggy Steinman, Rob Saba, Mark Hogan, and the owners of the Hall residence, who asked to remain anonymous. Thanks also to Tina Morris and other Soroptimist International volunteers who produce an excellent garden tour each July, and to Sue Beebe, assistant director of the Cornell Cooperative Extension of Saratoga County, for advice on local soil and climate.

The superb staff and resources of the Saratoga Public Library and the Saratoga Room, Victoria Garlanda and Teri Blasko, spent many hours patiently helping me find the answers to so many questions. Victoria went above and beyond her job in so many ways, and Teri's love of both history and gardening were a tremendous asset.

My appreciation also goes to Natalie Walsh, whom I met by chance at the library—a fortuitous event that led to a cherished personal and professional friendship.

Special thanks go to:

- Charlie Wheeler, facilities manager, and John Lee, former director of communications and media relations, at the Saratoga Race Course

- Kathy Locke, NYRA; Sally Nizolek, head gardener at the Saratoga Gaming and Raceway

- Mike Kane, former communications officer, and Allan Carter, historian, at the Saratoga Racing Museum

- Racing expert Dick Hamilton

- Bill Meisner, facilities manager at Fasig-Tipton

- Tom McTygue, former Saratoga Springs commissioner of public works; Rob Wheelock, head of the city beautification crew; James Gapczynski, former Flower Power director; and Stephanie Voight

- Dan Urkevich, head gardener, and Allison Schweizer and Donna Mannell in the administrative offices at Spa Park

- Michael Shadix, librarian at the Roosevelt Institute (Georgia)

- Greg Dixon, Saratoga County Chamber of Commerce

- Ed and Maureen Lewi, and Mark Bardack at Ed Lewi Associates

- Samantha Bosshart, executive director of the Saratoga Springs Preservation Foundation

- Wendy Anthony, curator of special collections, and Lauren Draus, librarian, at Skidmore College

- Florence Andresen, Skidmore Alumni Memorial Garden

- Anne Palamountain

- Edward Foley, head gardener, and Sarajane Brimhall, property manager, at Skidmore Apartments

Thank you to all the nursery/florist business owners and personnel who helped me: Charles "Dude" Dehn, Ned Chapman, Heather Chapman, Rich Morris, Gretchen Schrade Squires, Peter Saxton, Suzanne Balet Haight, Greg Greene, Dick Thayer, Cindy Behan, Kerry Mendez, Wynne Trowbridge, Melanie Mason, and designers Dick Thayer, Susie Kane-Kettlewell, and Robin Wolfe.

Thanks to those associated with Yaddo: Lesley Leduc, public affairs coordinator, and Jane Wait and Verena Takekoshi of the Yaddo Garden Association.

Thanks to the staff at the Brackett House: Donna Brayman and Joan Merboth; also Frank Oatman and Jon Wood.

Thanks also to the staff at the Batcheller Mansion: Bruce Levinsky, owner, Daniel DelGaudio, innkeeper, and Keyna Karp, gardener.

At the Union Gables B&B, I wish to thank Kelley Hamik and Thomas Van Gelder.

Special thanks go to Chauncey Olcott Johnstone, Paul Schrade, Kathryn Gallien, Gail Shapiro and Peter Fry, Bill Dorr, Joellen Unger, Twila Wolfe, Susan Johnson, Joe Deuel, and Yvonne Manso at the Pallette Stone Corporation.

I appreciate the expertise and advice provided by historians Field Horne and Ellen deLalla; Lynn Calvin at the Saratoga County Historical Society; Dr. Don Siegel, professor of earth sciences at Syracuse University; Curt Brandhorst, graphic design and computers; David Coennen, garden and history. Very special thanks to Sara Stennett, my Apple guru, who has patiently led me out of my comfort zone and into the infinitely perplexing world of digital photography and technology.

And a very heartfelt thanks to the Fagles, my second family, and my brother, Gary Loughrey, for giving me a home base.

An outdoor "living room" at the Hogan-Saba house.

Resources

Public Gardens

Skidmore Alumni Memorial Garden

Surrey Williamson Inn
815 North Broadway, Saratoga Springs, NY 12866
The garden looks best in summer and early fall.

Yaddo Gardens

Union Avenue, Saratoga Springs, NY 12866
(518) 584-0746; www.yaddo.org
The rose and shade gardens are open daily from spring to fall.
Most of the remaining estate is closed to the public to ensure the
resident artists' privacy.

Garden Resources

City of Saratoga Springs Public Compost program

City Hall
474 Broadway, Saratoga Springs, NY 12866
(518) 587-3550, ext. 2555 or 2623
High-quality soil amendment made from composted yard debris;
pH tested by Cornell Cooperative Extension for suitability for
home gardens. Available from April (varies from year to year)
until supplies are gone. Call for more information.

Cornell University Cooperative Extension of Saratoga County

50 West High Street, Ballston Spa, NY 12020
(518) 885-8995; www.ccesaratoga.org
Master Gardener hotline; information for soil testing and other
resources

Garden Clubs: Heritage Garden Club and Katrina Trask Garden Club

Updated contact information available at Federated Garden
Clubs of New York State website: www.gardencentral.org/fgcny

Secret Garden Tours, Soroptimist International of Saratoga County

Annual tour of some of Saratoga's finest gardens, held the second Sunday in July to raise money for this professional women's
organization. For further information, contact Saratoga Springs
Visitor Center (www.saratogatourism.com).

Seeds for Peace International, Inc.

Susan Johnson
PO Box 10, Saratoga Springs, NY 12866
www.seedsforpeace.net
Helps gardeners across the world grow their own food

Area Attractions and Resources

Fasig-Tipton Saratoga

East and Madison Avenue, Saratoga Springs, NY 12866
(518) 584-4700; www.fasigtipton.com
Yearling auction held in early August

National Museum of Racing and Hall of Fame

191 Union Avenue, Saratoga Springs, NY 12866
(518) 584-0400, (800) 562-5394; www.racingmuseum.org

Petrified Sea Gardens

Currently closed. For up-to-date information, call the local tourism bureau or contact D. A. Collins Companies (www.dacollins
.com).

Saratoga Farmers' Market

High Rock Avenue, Saratoga Springs, NY 12866
www.saratogafarmersmarket.org
Seasonal outdoor market each Wednesday (3 to 6 p.m.) and
Saturday (9 a.m. to 1 p.m.) from spring to fall; indoor winter
market

Saratoga Gaming and Raceway

Crescent Avenue, Saratoga Springs, NY 12866
(518) 584-2110; www.saratogagamingandraceway.com
Harness track and casino

Saratoga Race Course

Union Avenue, Saratoga Springs, NY 12866
(518) 584-6200; www.nyra.com/Saratoga/

Saratoga Spa State Park

19 Roosevelt Drive, Saratoga Springs, NY 12866
(518) 584-2535; www.saratogaspastatepark.org

Saratoga Springs Heritage Visitor Center

297 Broadway, Saratoga Springs, NY 12866
(518) 587-3241; www.saratogatourism.com
A former trolley building with a welcome garden and history displays

Nurseries, Florists, Garden Centers

Balet Flowers & Design

Suzanne Balet Haight
5041 Nelson Avenue Extension, Malta, NY 12020
(518) 584-8555; www.baletflowers.com
Floral design, seasonal nursery, and farmers' market vendor

Dehn's Flowers & Greenhouses, Inc.

180 Beekman Street, Saratoga Springs, NY 12866
(518) 584-1880 or (800) 932-0933; www.dehnsflowers.com
Full-service florist and nursery

Saxton Gardens

Peter Saxton
First Street, Saratoga Springs, NY 12866
(518) 584-4697
Specialty grower of hybridized daylilies, including 'Adirondack Strain'

Schrade's Posie Peddler

Gretchen Schrade Squires and Jim Squires
32 Congress Street, Saratoga Springs, NY 12866
(518) 587-8273; www.posiepeddler.com
Custom arrangements for special occasions

Sunnyside Gardens

345 Church Street, Saratoga Springs, NY 12866
(518) 584-1034; www.chapmansunnysidegardens.com
Full-service retail nursery and garden center

Toadflax Nursery

1604 Saratoga Road, South Glens Falls, NY 12803
(518) 793-2886; www.toadflaxnursery.com
Full-service retail nursery; also offers garden design, consultation, and installation

Garden Design

Behan Planning and Design

Cindy Behan, landscape architect
112 Spring Street, Suite 305, Saratoga Springs, NY 12866
(518) 583-4335; www.behanplanning.com
Community planning; commercial and residential landscapes

Garden Masters

Susie Kane-Kettlewell
(518) 695-4320; cell (518) 791-4113
Consultations; perennials a specialty

Perennially Yours

Kerry and Sergio Mendez
P.O. Box 144, Ballston Spa, NY 12020
(518) 885-3471
www.pyours.com
Lectures, garden consultations, workshops, and open gardens

Saratoga Landscape Company

Dick Thayer
PO Box 4535, Saratoga Springs, NY 12866
(518) 581-1413; www.saratogalandscape.com
Design, consultation, installation; specializing in trees and shrubs

Wild Ginger Designs

Greg Greene
13 Northup Drive, Queensbury, NY 12804
(518) 792-5934
Design, consultation, installation; specializing in woodland shade plants